The Royal Court presents

East is East

by Ayub Khan-Din

Produced by Tamasha Theatre Company, the Royal Court Theatre Company and Birmingham Repertory Company.

First performance at Birmingham Repertory Studio Theatre 8 October 1996.
First performance at the Royal Court Theatre Upstairs 19 November 1996.
First performance at the Royal Court Theatre Downstairs 26 March 1997.

The Royal Court Theatre is financially assisted by the Royal Borough of Kensington and Chelsea. Recipient of a grant from the Theatre Restoration Fund & from the Foundation for Sport & the Arts. The Royal Court's Play Development Programme is funded by the Audrey Skirball-Kenis Theatre. Supported by the National Lottery through the Arts Council of England. Royal Court Registered Charity number 231242.
Tamasha Registered Charity number 1001483.
Birmingham Repertory Theatre 223660.

The English Stage Company at the Royal Court Theatre

The English Stage Company was formed to bring serious writing back to the stage. The first Artistic Director, George Devine, wanted to create a vital and popular theatre. He encouraged new writing that explored subjects drawn from contemporary life as well as pursuing European plays and forgotten classics. When John Osborne's **Look Back in Anger** was first produced in 1956, it forced British Theatre into the modern age. In addition to plays by "angry young men", the international repertoire ranged from Brecht to Ionesco, by way of Jean-Paul Sartre, Marguerite Duras, Wedekind and Beckett.

The ambition was to discover new work which was challenging, innovative and also of the highest quality, underpinned by the desire to discover a contemporary style of presentation. Early Court writers included Arnold Wesker, John Arden, David Storey, Ann Jellicoe, N F Simpson and Edward Bond. They were followed by David Hare and Howard Brenton, Caryl Churchill, Timberlake Wertenbaker, Robert Holman and Jim Cartwright. Many of their plays are now regarded as modern classics.

Many established playwrights had their early plays produced in the Theatre Upstairs including Anne Devlin, Andrea Dunbar, Sarah Daniels, Jim Cartwright, Clare McIntyre, Winsome Pinnock, Martin Crimp and Phyllis Nagy. Since 1994 there has been a major season of plays by writers new to the Royal Court, many of them first plays, produced in association with the *Royal National Theatre Studio* with sponsorship from *The Jerwood Foundation*. The writers include Joe Penhall, Nick Grosso, Judy Upton, Sarah Kane, Michael Wynne, Judith Johnson, James Stock, Simon Block and Mark Ravenhill. In 1996-97 the Jerwood Foundation sponsored the Jerwood New Playwrights season, a series of six plays by Jez Butterwoth and Martin McDonagh (in the Theatre Downstairs), Mark Ravenhill, Ayub Khan-Din, Tamantha Hammerschlag and Jess Walters (in the Theatre Upstairs).

Theatre Upstairs productions have regularly transferred to the Theatre Downstairs, as with Ariel Dorfman's **Death and the Maiden**, Sebastian Barry's **The Steward of Christendom**, a co-production with *Out of Joint*, and Martin McDonagh's **The Beauty Queen Of Leenane,** a co-production with Druid Theatre Company. Some Theatre Upstairs productions have transferred to the West End, most recently with Kevin Elyot's **My Night With Reg** at the Criterion.

1992-1996 have been record-breaking years at the box-office with capacity houses for productions of **Faith Healer, Death and the Maiden, Six Degrees of Separation, King Lear, Oleanna, Hysteria, Cavalcaders, The Kitchen, The Queen & I, The Libertine, Simpatico, Mojo** and **The Steward of Christendom**.

Death and the Maiden and **Six Degrees of Separation** won the Olivier Award for Best Play in 1992 and 1993 respectively. **Hysteria** won the 1994 Olivier Award for Best Comedy, and also the Writers' Guild Award for Best West End Play. **My Night with Reg** won the 1994 Writers' Guild Award for Best Fringe Play, the Evening Standard Award for Best Comedy, and the 1994 Olivier Award for Best Comedy. Jonathan Harvey won the 1994 Evening Standard Drama Award for Most Promising Playwright, for **Babies**. Sebastian Barry won the 1995 Writers' Guild Award for Best Fringe Play for **The Steward of Christendom** and also the 1995 Lloyds Private Banking Playwright of the Year Award. Jez Butterworth won the 1995 George Devine Award for Most Promising Playwright, the 1995 Writers' Guild New Writer of the Year, the Evening Standard Award for Most Promising Newcomer and the 1995 Olivier Award for Best Comedy for **Mojo**. Phyllis Nagy won the 1995 Writers' Guild Award for Best Regional Play for **Disappeared**. Martin McDonagh won the 1996 George Devine Award for Most Promising Playwright, the 1996 Writers' Guild Best Fringe Play Award, and the 1996 Evening Standard Drama Award for Most Promising Newcomer for **The Beauty Queen of Leenane**. The Royal Court won the 1995 Prudential Award for the Theatre, and was the overall winner of the 1995 Prudential Award for the Arts for creativity, excellence, innovation and accessibility. The Royal Court won the 1995 Peter Brook Empty Space Award for innovation and excellence in theatre.

Now in its temporary homes The Duke Of York's and Ambassadors Theatres, during the two-year refurbishment of its Sloane Square theatre, the Royal Court continues to present the best in new work. After four decades the company's aims remain consistent with those established by George Devine. The Royal Court is still a major focus in the country for the production of new work. Scores of plays first seen at the Royal Court are now part of the national and international dramatic repertoire.

Tamasha Theatre Company

Tamasha was formed in 1989 by Sudha Bhuchar and Kristine Landon-Smith to adapt **UNTOUCHABLE**, a classic Indian novel by Mulk Raj Anand. After an extremely successful debut the company has gone from strength to strength having produced 6 plays, 4 of which have been adapted for broadcast on Radio 4, and having collaborated with theatres such as the Royal Court, Birmingham Repertory, Bristol Old Vic, and Theatre Royal, Stratford East.

The company's style of research and production with its emphasis on authenticity now has a large and growing following: both the Asian and general British theatre going public. **Tamasha** aims to reflect through theatre the Asian experience - from British Asian life to authentic accounts of aspects of life in the Indian sub continent, adapting works of literature and classics to commissioning new work from a range of contemporary writers.

The millennium marks Tamasha's 10th anniversary and our plan is to begin the 21st century as a full time company with Arts Council franchise funding and housed in our own building with rehearsal and office facilities. This would enable Tamasha to be at the forefront of the development of a culturally diverse British Theatre. To this end a 3 year fundraising campaign was launched on 31st August 1996. If you are interested in sponsorship opportunities with the company please contact:
Anne Louise Wirgman, 184 Victoria Road, London N22 4XQ. Tel/Fax 0181 889 6432

14 August 1997 marks the 50th anniversary of the partition of India into India and Pakistan and the end of Brirtish rule in India. This was one of the largest explusions of people from their homes ever to take place in history, with millions of Hindus and Muslims fleeing accross the border in opposite directions in fear for their lives. People who had lived side by side for centuries turned against each other spurred on by the British "divide and rule" policy.

Tamasha's production for 1997 will be **PARTITION** (working title) a new play whihc we have commissioned from Harwant Baines, the award-winning writer of feature film WILD WEST and BBC2's TWO ORANGES AND A MANGO. We are delighted to have been invited to open the production as part of the 1997 Edinburgh International Festival at the Gateway Theatre, 11th-18th August.

Tamasha's project will look at the personal face pf partition, the legacy left behind after the events of August 1947. How the generation which did not live through the events are still haunted by the wounds of 1947. Is partition a scar that has never healed and what is the effect on the Asian community in Britian even further removed from the event - they too are not immune to its effect. Young Asians contemplating mixed religion relationships all too often find that love does not conquer all and they have to face deep set views and prejudices about each other's community. Teenagers take pride in definining themselves through religious communities. Are they fanning the fire begun in 1947?

TAMASHA PAST PRODUCTIONS
1989 **UNTOUCHABLE**
based on a novel by Mulk Raj Anand
1991 **HOUSE OF THE SUN**
based on the novel by Meira Chand
1992 **WOMEN OF THE DUST**
by Ruth Carter
1993 **WOMEN OF THE DUST**
by Ruth Carter on tour to India
1994 **A SHAFT OF SUNLIGHT**
by Abhijat Joshi
1995 **A YEARNING**
based on Lorca's YERMA, by Ruth Carter

For further information on Tamasha contact:
Sudha Bhuchar or Kristine Landon-Smith,
Joint Artistic Directors, 184 Victoria Road,
N22 4XQ. Tel: 0181 889 6432
Tamasha Board:
Ajay Bhuchar, Joel Levy,
Asif Mahmud (Chair), Cal McCrystal,
Lisbeth Savill, Vinod Tailor.
Tamasha Advisory Committee:
Bill Alexander, Kamlesh Bahl, Stephen Daldry,
Baroness Flather, Saeed Jaffrey OBE, Art
Malik, G K Noon MBE, Zohra Segal.

For Tamasha Theatre Company

Joint Artistic Directors **Sudha Bhuchar**
Kristine Landon-Smith
Press and Marketing **Suman Bhuchar**
Administrator **Anne Louise Wirgman**

BIRMINGHAM REPERTORY THEATRE COMPANY

Following the great success of **A SHAFT OF SUNLIGHT** and **A YEARNING**, **EAST IS EAST** is the third collaboration between Birmingham Repertory Theatre Company and Tamasha Theatre Company.

Birmingham Repertory Theatre Company is one of Britain's major producing theatres, led by Artistic Director, Bill Alexander. It is committed to producing classic plays, discovering plays and new work. The company creates around 14 productions each year which are produced for both Main Stage and Studio.

Increasingly the company's work is seen by a much wider audience on tour (as in the case of **A SHAFT OF SUNLIGHT** in 1994 and **A YEARNING** last year) or by productions transferring to London. Recently four Birmingham Repertory Theatre Company productions have been seen on the London stage: **LADY WINDERMERE'S FAN**, Albery Theatre; **ONCE ON THIS ISLAND**, Island Theatre; **A VIEW FROM THE BRIDGE**, Strand Theatre; and **THE IMPORTANCE OF BEING EARNEST**, Old Vic. This autumn, Birmingham Repertory Theatre Company and the Royal National Theatre have joined forces for the first time and co-produced Ben Jonson's **THE ALCHEMIST**. Directed by Bill Alexander, the production opened at the Olivier Theatre on 8th October 1996 following a sell out run at Birmingham.

Birmingham Repertory Theatre Company also has a commitment to produce work for the widest possible audience. The company seeks to ensure that its work is culturally diverse, appealing to as many different communities as possible.

We are also active in the fields of education, community, youth and outreach work. It pursues a vigorous programme of education and community work which challenges and extends the range of Main House and Studio productions.

Birmingham Repertory Theatre Company is one of Birmingham's major arts organisations which have made the city famous nationally and internationally for the quality of its artistic endeavour.

DIVERSE ACTS

was set up by London Arts Board to respond to new work and initiatives emerging from communities and individuals originating in the Caribbean, Indian sub-continent, China, Africa, the Pacific Rim and Latin America. The very first award under this scheme goes to Tamasha Theatre Company for **EAST IS EAST**.

TAMASHA THEATRE COMPANY and NEW WRITING

EAST IS EAST by Ayub Khan-Din was developed in a writers' workshop that Tamasha held in January 1996, in collaboration with the Royal Court. This is the first time we have been able to hold a workshop outside a production to offer training to professionals of a particular discipline. Last year's workshop was possible through the assistance of London Arts Board and The Peggy Ramsay Foundation.

For two weeks writers were tutored by Harwant Bains, Elyse Dodgson, Kristine Landon-Smith, Carl Miller, Phyllis Nagy, Winsome Pinnock and Ian Rickson, on all aspects of writing for theatre. We also looked at the many different ways of developing new work. Each writer then workshopped a piece of work with actors, director and dramaturg and **EAST IS EAST** was one of those works.

It is mainly with the assistance of London Arts Board and their new award **DIVERSE ACTS** that we are able to pursue this line of work. And it is very important that we do, so that a greater volume of work from writers of Asian origin comes through, as there are still so many stories yet untold.

EAST IS EAST is one of those stories. This is the first play to be produced on the British stage that really gets under the skin of what it is to be of mixed race origin within the Asian community, growing up in a culture that is predominantly working class British. Both worlds (England and Pakistan) inevitably influence the characters in the play, and for us **EAST IS EAST** shows that identities forged out of those backgrounds are multifarious and that it is not just simply a question of East versus West. We hope you enjoy it.

Sudha Bhuchar, Kristine Landon-Smith
Joint Artistic Directors, Tamasha Theatre Company

JERWOOD
NEW PLAYWRIGHTS

Jerwood New Playwrights sees the Jerwood Foundation coming forward for a second year as a major sponsor of the Royal Court Theatre. This series of six plays staged in the winter and spring of 1996-7, will be a notable celebration of the best of contemporary playwriting. Certain of the plays reached the Royal Court stage last year, to great acclaim: **Mojo** by Jez Butterworth and **The Beauty Queen of Leenane** by Martin McDonagh. Together with four premieres of first plays this underlines still further the notable importance of the Royal Court as a forcing ground for new talent.

I am a great admirer of the exceptionally high artistic level the Royal Court has achieved. This achievement fits perfectly with the ideals of the Jerwood Foundation, a private foundation established in 1977 by the late John Jerwood. It is dedicated to imaginative and responsible funding and sponsorship of the arts, education, design, conservation, medicine, science and engineering, and of other areas of human endeavour and excellence.

The Foundation is increasingly known for its support of the arts. In the field of the visual arts, two major awards are increasingly bringing it to public attention. The first is the Jerwood Painting Prize, now in its third year and the most valuable art prize in the United Kingdom. The second is the Jerwood Foundation Prize for Applied Arts, the largest prize of its kind in Europe, which in 1996 was offered for ceramics.
The Council of the Foundation has singled out one particular strand for development within the Foundation's varied field of benefactors: support of talented young people who have persevered in their chosen

career and will benefit from the financial support and recognition which will launch them. To achieve this goal, a number of awards and sponsorships have been developed in concert with organisations such as the Royal Ballet Companies (for the Jerwood Young Choreographers Awards); the National Film and Television School; the Royal Academy of Dancing; and The Royal Academy of Engineering.

The Foundation sponsors the Brereton International Music Symposium which gives masterclasses for young professional windplayers and singers, the National Youth Chamber Orchestra, and the Opera and Music Theatre Lab at Bore Place in Kent. In 1996, with The Big Issue it co-sponsored The Big Screening, a free season of new films by British directors. Across all the arts, it is vital that financial support is given to the creation of new work. It is for this simple reason that we are delighted to be sponsoring another exciting season with the Royal Court.

Alan Grieve
Chairman

Jerwood New Playwrights

10 October - 9 November 1996
Mojo
by Jez Butterworth
26 September - 19 October 1996
Shopping and F£££ing
by Mark Ravenhill
25 November - 7 December 1996
East is East
by Ayub Khan-Din
29 November 1996 - 11 January 1997
The Beauty Queen of Leenane
by Martin McDonagh
6 February - 1 March 1997
Backpay
by Tamantha Hammerschlag
3 February - 1 March 1997
Cockroach, Who?
by Jess Walters

EAST IS EAST

by Ayub Khan-Din

Cast

George Khan	Nasser Memarzia
Ella Khan *(his wife)*	Linda Bassett

Their children:

Abdul	Paul Bazely
Tariq	Jimi Mistry
Maneer	Emil Marwa
Saleem	Chris Bisson
Meena	Zita Sattar
Sajit	Imran Ali
Auntie Annie *(friend of Ella's)*	Gillian Hanna
Doctor/Mr Shah	Kriss Dosanjh

Director	Kristine Landon-Smith
Designer	Sue Mayes
Lighting Designer	Paul Taylor
Dialect Coach	Jill McCullough
Fight Director	Malcolm Ransom
Education Consultant	Becky Chapman
Tour Production Manager	Dennis Charles
Production Manager (Royal Court)	Edwyn Wilson
Stage Manager	Lisa Buckley
Stage Manager	Jonathan Smith-Howard
Production Photographs	Robert Day
Set built by	Birmingham Repertory Theatre Company

The play is set in 1970's Salford.

Thanks To: David Lan, all the participants of the Writers Workshop Fortnight, Deepa Patel, Vijay Bhuchar, Clare Cooper, The Paul Hamlyn Foundation, The Esmée Fairbairn Charitable Trust, Cafe Lazeez for London Press Night, Shaheen Khan, Ron Stenner at "Casts" - medical services to the media for the loan of the stethoscope and wheelchair, Hairways (Edmonton) Ltd for the loan of the barbers chair, Metcalfe Catering Equipment Ltd for the loan of the chipper, Honeyrose Products Ltd, Reckitt's Heritage, Cigarette Packet Collectors Club of Great Britain, Rajah Indian Foods, Shimla Pinks.

Ayub Khan-Din (Writer)

This is Ayub's first play.

As an actor, theatre includes: The Little Clay Cart, The Story's Not For Telling, Anklets of Fire (Tara Arts); Film, Film, Film (Act); Borderline (Nuffield Theatre, Southampton); Poppy (Half Moon); Tartuffe (RNT).

Television includes: London Bridge, Coronation Street, My Family and Other Animals, Shalom, Salaam Back Up, Dangerfield, Staying Alive

Film includes: My Beautiful Launderette, Sammy & Rosie Get Laid, Farewell Stranger, The Burning Season, The Idiot. Work in progress: Achaa, Rifat Woz 'ere, Last Dance at Dum-Dum.

Imran Ali

Theatre includes: The Great Hale (Reamould Theatre Company); The Rose, Oliver Twist (Bridlington Theatre Company); Summer in the Empire (The Spa Theatre).

Film includes: North China Lover.

Linda Bassett

For the Royal Court: The Recruiting Officer, Our Country's Good, Serious Money (also Wyndhams and New York), Aunt Dan and Lemon (also New York), Abel's Sister.

Other theatre includes: The Clearing (Bush Theatre); Henry IV 1&2, The Theban Plays, Artists and Admirers (RSC); The Awakening (Hampstead); Schism in England, A Place with the Pigs, Juno and the Paycock (RNT); The Seagull (Liverpool Playhouse); The Cherry Orchard, Medea, The Bald Prima Donna (Leicester Haymarket); Fen (Joint Stock); work with Coventry TIE Company and Interplay Community Theatre.

TV includes: Bramwell, Frank Stubbs Promotes, Kavanagh QC, Loved Up, Cold Light of Day, Skallagrig, No Bananas, Casualty, Traffic, The Bill, A Small Dance, A Touch of Frost, Boon.

Film includes: A Village Affair, Mary Reilly, Newshounds, Waiting for the Moon, Indian Summer, Oscar and Lucinda.

Paul Bazely

Theatre includes: Brother Eichmann, Beauty and the Beast (Library Theatre, Manchester); Macbeth (Full Company); Soldiers, The Big Heart (Contact Theatre, Manchester); Richard III (RNT and USA tour); Selling Out (The Old Fire Station, Oxford); Tomfoolery, Cigarettes and Chocolate, Selling Out, Bye Bye Blues (Stephen Joseph Theatre, Scarborough); Seed (Lyric Hammersmith); Peter Pan, Toad of Toad Hall (Birmingham Rep); The Servant of Two Masters (Sheffield Crucible).

Television includes: Casualty, Wuthering Heights, Making Out, Resnick, Emmerdale, Medics, New Voices, The Quiet Lifer.

Radio includes: The Maneater of Malgudi, No Problem, Resnick.

Chris Bisson

Theatre includes: A Streetcar Named Desire (Chapman Theatre, Salford); Badenheim 1939 (Adelphi Theatre, Salford); Dr Faustus, The Lower Depths (The Green Room); Fame is the Spur (Library Theatre, Manchester).

Television includes: Prime Suspect 5, Circle of Deceit, Express, The 8-15 from Manchester, Childrens Ward.

Kriss Dosanjh

Theatre includes: Lost for Words, Crossed Lines (New Focus Theatre Co); Sharazad (Oxford Touring Co); The Rainbow Bird (Keeping Mum Theatre Co).

Television includes: Broker's Man, Virtual Murder, Specials, Vote for Them, Crimewatch UK, Family Pride, Family Pride, The Zero Option.

Films include: Turning World, Guru in Seven.

Radio includes: Not All Angels Have Wings, The Little Clay Cart, The Tiger, House of the Sun, Untouchable.

Gillian Hanna

For the Royal Court: Hot Fudge and Ice Cream, The Queen and I (and Out of Joint).

Theatre includes: Who's Afraid of Virginia Woolf, A Common Woman, Duet for One (Sheffield Crucible); Curtains (Hampstead); Love Story of the Century (Monstrous Regiment); Juno and the Paycock (Contact Theatre); Wallflowering (West Yorkshire Playhouse); Romeo and Juliet, A View From the Bridge (Royal Exchange, Manchester); Big Maggie (Birmingham Rep); An Ideal Husband (Salisbury

Playhouse); The Entertainer (Birmingham Rep and West Yorkshire Playhouse); The House of Bernarda Alba (Theatr Clwyd). Television includes: The Heart Surgeon, Casualty, Drop the Dead Donkey, Brookside, Desmonds, The Philip Knight Story, The House of Bernarda Alba. Film includes: The Woman of The Wolf, Wolves of Willoughby Chase.

Kristine Landon-Smith (director),

Graduated from The Royal Scottish Academy of Music and Drama in 1981. As an actress Kristine has worked all over Britain with companies including The Royal Court Theatre; Hull Truck Theatre Company; Theatr Clwyd; Durham Theatre; Theatre Royal Stratford East and Tara Arts. In 1985 she co-founded The Inner Circle Theatre Company, and in 1989 she and Sudha Bhuchar co-founded Tamasha Theatre Company. She is currently a producer for BBC Radio Drama.
For Tamasha, theatre includes: Untouchable (Riverside Studios, London and national tour); House of the Sun (Stratford East); Women of the Dust (Riverside Studios and national tour of India), A Shaft of Sunlight (Birmingham Rep and national tour), A Yearning (Lyric Hammersmith and national tour).
Other theatre includes: Spring Awakening (Young Vic), Bodycount, Yerma (Bristol Old Vic).
Radio includes: Uganda, House by the River, Change of Heart.
Kristine's most recent project Capricornia was a co-production with the BBC and the Austrailian Broadcasting Company and was recorded in Perth, Austrailia.

Nasser Memarzia

For the Royal Court: Cry With Sewn Lips, Prometheus in Erin.
Other theatre includes: Hiawatha (Bristol Old Vic); How the Other Half Loves (Theatre Royal, Northampton); Deborah's Daughter (Library Theatre, Manchester); I Miss My War (Almeida).
Television includes: Leave to Remain, The Bill, Children's Ward, Flight Terminal, Casualty, Between the Lines.
As a writer his work for the stage includes: On the Rocks, All Dressed Up (Yorkshire Theatre Company); Two Tone (Pilot Theatre Company); A Timeless Time (Alive and Kicking Theatre Company); Dusky Warriors (Co-written, Theatre Royal Stratford East - LWT Awards 1995). He also co-wrote Breath of Life, a short film nominated for a BAFTA in 1993. Currently working on a film adaptation of Dusky Warriors with co-writer Kulvinder Ghir.

Emil Marwa

Theatre includes: Gift (White Bear Theatre); Simple Past (The Gate); Gum and Goo (The Bird's Nest).
Television includes: Grange Hill, Eastenders.

Jimi Mistry

Television includes: Thieftakers.
Film includes: Hamlet.
He has also taken part in a number of new writing workshops at the Royal Court. This is his first professional role since graduating from drama school.

Sue Mayes (Designer)

Trained at the Central School of Art and Design and began her designing career at Ipswich Repertory. Since then she has worked extensively around the country with residences at Coventry Belgrade TIE; Contact Theatre, Manchester; and The Liverpool Everyman. As a freelance designer her work has included productions for: Tynewear Theatre Company; The Traverse Theatre, Edinburgh; New Victoria Theatre, Stoke on Trent, and Graeae Theatre company.
Recent designs for theatre include: Quilt (The Oval House); Waterfall (Moving Theatre, Riverside Studios); Jack and the Beanstalk (Theatre Royal Stratford East); Zebra Crossing (Talawa Theatre Company, Young Vic); Maid Marion and her Merry Men (costumes, Bristol Old Vic).
Sue has designed all previous Tamasha productions.

Zita Sattar

Theatre includes: Up 'n Gone (Birmingham Rep Studio); Roadrunners (Midlands Arts Centre), Top Girls (Northampton); D'yer Eat With Your Fingers? (Theatre Royal Stratford East); A Yearning (Tamasha Theatre Company).
Television includes: Y.E.S, The Bill, The Hale and Pace Show, Back Up.
Radio includes: A Yearning, Girlies,

Change of Heart, The Stones of Mancaster Castle.

Paul Taylor (lighting designer).
Design for theatre includes: Betrayal (Citizens Theatre, Glasgow); Dusky Warriors (Stratford East); Death Catches the Hunter (Battersea Arts Centre); A Yearning (Tamasha Theatre Company, Birmingham Rep and Lyric Hammersmith); Cabaret (Theatre Hagen, Germany).
Design for opera includes: Terrible Mouth, Mario and the Magician (Almeida Theatre); Griselidis (Guildhall School of Music and Drama); The Garden (Donmar Warehouse); Don Giovanni (Music Theatre, London); The Marriage of Figaro, Don Giovanni (Surrey Opera); Beauty (Theatre Hagen, Germany).
He has also worked with The Vienna State Opera, The Netherlands Opera, English National Opera, and Welsh National Opera.
Design for dance and ballet includes: Swan Lake (Wiesbaden Ballet), Sleeping Beauty (Hanover Ballet); Don Quixote (Northern Ballet), and works for Ballet Theatre Hagen, Tanz-Forum, Cologne, and the Ballet National de Nancy, France.
Currently working on The Servant of Two Masters (Theatre Clwyd, Nottingham Playhouse).

The Royal Court would like to thank the following for their help with this production:Wardrobe care by Persil and Comfort courtesy of Lever Brothers Ltd, refrigerators by Electrolux and Philips Major Appliances Ltd.; kettles for rehearsals by Morphy Richards; video for casting purposes by Hitachi; backstage coffee machine by West 9; furniture by Knoll International; freezer for backstage use supplied by Zanussi Ltd 'Now that's a good idea.' Hair styling by Carole at Moreno, 2 Holbein Place, Sloane Square 0171- 730-0211; Closed circuit TV cameras and monitors by Mitsubishi UK Ltd. Natural spring water from Wye Spring Water, 149 Sloane Street, London SW1, tel. 0171-730 6977. Overhead projector from W.H. Smith; Sanyo U.K for the backstage microwave.

How the Royal Court is brought to you

The Royal Court (English Stage Company Ltd) is supported financially by a wide range of public bodies and private companies, as well as its own trading activities. The company receives its principal funding from the **Arts Council of England**, which has supported the Royal Court since 1956. The **Royal Borough of Kensington & Chelsea** gives an annual grant to the Royal Court Young People's Theatre. The **London Boroughs Grants Committee** contributes to the cost of productions in the Theatre Upstairs.

Other parts of the company's activities are made possible by business sponsorships. Several of these sponsors have made a long-term commitment. 1996 saw the sixth Barclays New Stages Festival of Independent Theatre, supported throughout by **Barclays Bank**. **British Gas North Thames** supported three years of the Royal Court's Education Programme. Sponsorship by **WH Smith** helped to make the launch of the Friends of the Royal Court scheme so successful.

1993 saw the start of our association with the **Audrey Skirball-Kenis Theatre** of Los Angeles, which is funding a Playwrights Programme at the Royal Court. Exchange visits for writers between Britain and the USA complement the greatly increased programme of readings and play development which have fortified the company's capability to develop writing for the theatre nationally and internationally.

In 1988 the **Olivier Building Appeal** was launched, to raise funds to begin the task of restoring, repairing and improving the Royal Court Theatre, Sloane Square. This was made possible by a large number of generous supporters and significant contributions from the **Theatres Restoration Fund**, the **Rayne Foundation**, the **Foundation for Sport and the Arts** and the **Arts Council's Incentive Funding Scheme**.

The Company earns the rest of the money it needs to operate from the Box Office, from other trading and from transfers to the West End of plays such as **Death and the Maiden**, **Six Degrees of Separation**, **Oleanna** and **My Night With Reg**. But without public subsidy it would close immediately and its unique place in British theatre would be lost. If you care about the future of arts in this country, please write to your MP and say so.

Stage Hands Appeal

Royal Court Theatre

The history of the Royal Court Theatre, Sloane Square, is one of survival. Harley Granville Barker during his famous 1904-7 stewardship described the building as 'frightful'. George Devine thought it 'too small, too restricted'. Successive artistic directors, artists and managers have all bemoaned the appalling conditions yet, in spite of it all, have managed to create one of the most important theatrical legends of the British theatre.

Each generation has fiddled with the Royal Court Theatre's physical bearings: the 1888 structure was altered in 1921, bombed in the blitz, rebuilt in 1952, altered in 1954, messed about with in 1964, designed but never rebuilt in 1967 and repainted with the same brown every ten years or so.

By the summer of 1996 the very fabric of Theatre was crumbling and without immediate structural repairs we would have been forced to close. For good.

The advent of the National Lottery, and a subsequent lottery award to the Royal Court, has meant a partial rescue. But there's a twist in the tale.

The Royal Court hasn't yet been given the award and Lottery money will only be released if we can raise almost £6 million ourselves as partnership funding. We aim to raise over £5 million from businesses, charitable trusts and sponsorship deals. From the public, from friends and theatre-goers, we must raise £500,000. Without this help we'll lose the lot.

Our two-year building project is just beginning in Sloane Square. By contributing to the Stage Hands Appeal you can support the project: a £5 donation towards the appeal will pay for around 10 bricks while a gift of £25 will help secure the theatre's foundations, paying for half a cubic metre of concrete. And the way in which the Lottery Award works is that every £1 donated effectively 'unlocks' £3 of lottery money, so a donation of £25 actually results in the theatre receiving £100.

Early fundraising has already raised more than £150,000 which is a great start, but we need to continue this success. Leaflets giving more information about the Appeal are available from the Box Office in both the Theatre Downstairs and Theatre Upstairs, Stage Hands T-shirts are on sale for £10 from the Bookshop in the Theatre Downstairs and from the Bar in the Theatre Upstairs, and there is a replica model of the new-look Royal Court - which doubles up as a donation box - in the foyer of the Theatre Downstairs.

At a time when we are witnessing an extraordinary resurgence of creative energy in our Theatre it is vital that the Royal Court has a building that can meet the needs of writers, directors and audiences in full.

For further details please call 0171-930-4253.

Stage Hands Appeal

Invest in the future of New Theatre
Call 0171 930 4253

TRUSTS AND FOUNDATIONS
The Baring Foundation
The Campden Charities
John Cass's Foundation
The Chase Charity
The Esmeé Fairbairn
 Charitable Trust
The Robert Gavron
 Charitable Trust
Paul Hamlyn Foundation
The Jerwood Foundation
The John Lyons' Charity
The Mercers' Charitable
 Foundation
The Prince's Trust
Peggy Ramsay Foundation
The Rayne Foundation
The Lord Sainsbury
 Foundation for Sport & the
 Arts
The Wates Foundation

SPONSORS
AT&T
Barclays Bank
Hugo Boss
Brunswick PR Ltd
Citibank
The Evening Standard
The Granada Group Plc
John Lewis Partnership
Marks & Spencer Plc
The New Yorker
Prudential Corporation Plc
W H Smith

CORPORATE PATRONS
Advanpress
Associated Newspapers
 Ltd
Bunzl Plc
Citigate Communications
Criterion Productions Plc
Dibb Lupton Alsop

Homevale Ltd
Laporte Plc
Lazard Brothers & Co. Ltd
Lex Service Plc
The Mirror Group Plc
New Penny Productions
 Ltd
Noel Gay Artists/Hamilton
Asper Management
A T Poeton & Son Ltd
The Simkins Partnership
Simons Muirhead and
 Burton
Deloitte & Touche

PATRONS
Sir Christopher Bland
Greg Dyke
Spencer & Calla Fleischer
Barbara Minto
Greville Poke
Richard Pulford
Sir George Russell
Richard Wilson

ASSOCIATES
Nicholas A Fraser
Patricia Marmont

BENEFACTORS
Mr & Mrs Gerry Acher
David H. Adams
Bill Andrewes
Batia Asher
Elaine Attias
Angela Bernstein
Jeremy Bond
Julia Brodie
Julian Brookstone
Guy Chapman
Yuen-Wei Chew
Carole & Neville Conrad
Conway van Gelder
Coppard Fletcher & Co.
Lisa Crawford Irwin
Curtis Brown Ltd
Louise & Brian Cuzner
Allan Davis
Robert Dufton
Robyn Durie
Gill Fitzhugh
Kim Fletcher & Sarah Sands
Winston Fletcher
Norman Gerard
Henny Gestetner OBE
Jules Goddard
Carolyn Goldbart
Rocky Gottlieb
Stephen Gottlieb

Frank & Judy Grace
Jan Harris
Angela Heylin
Andre Hoffman
Chris Hopson
Jane How & Richard Durden
Institute of Practitioners
 in Advertising
International Creative
 Management
Jarvis Hotels
Peter Jones
Sahra Lese
Judy Lever
Lady Lever
Sally Margulies
Pat Morton
Michael Orr
Sir Eric Parker
Lynne Pemberton
Carol Rayman
Angharad Rees
B J & Rosemary Reynolds
John Sandoe (Books) Ltd
Scott Tallon Walker
Nicholas Selmes
Maria Shammas
Lord Sheppard
Dr Gordon Taylor
Tomkins Plc
A P Thompson
Eric Walters
A P Watt Ltd
Sue Weaver, The Sloane Club
Nick Wilkinson

AMERICAN FRIENDS
Patrons
Miriam Blenstock
Tina Brown
Caroline Graham
Richard & Marcia Grand
Ann & Mick Jones
Maurie Perl
Rhonda Sherman

Members
Monica Gerard-Sharp
Linda S. Lese
Yasmine Lever
Enid W. Morse
Mr & Mrs Frederick Rose
Paul & Daisy Soros

Many thanks to all our supporters for their vital and on-going commitment

EAST IS EAST

To Hilda, Charlie, and all at 63

2

Cast

GEORGE KHAN, father, 55
ELLA KHAN, mother, 46
ABDUL KHAN, son, 23
TARIQ KHAN, son, 21
MANEER KHAN, son, 19
SALEEM KHAN, son, 18
MEENAH KHAN, daughter, 16
SAJIT KHAN, son, 12
AUNTIE ANNIE, 50
MR SHAH, 52

Act One, Scene One

The action takes place in Salford in 1970, prior to the outbreak of war between India and Pakistan over the independence of East Pakistan. The KHANS are an Anglo-Pakistani family of eight. The contrast of cultures should come out in the set dressing, wallpaper, oil cloth, Islamic prayer stickers, a coffee table with a picture of the Taj Mahal, a Lazy Susan which is always full of washing.

The set is made up of a fish and chip shop, a parlour, living room, and a kitchen with a shed attached. The parlour should be more up market as it's used for entertaining. When the play begins we find ELLA and ANNIE sat in the living room talking, drinking tea and smoking. They're very good friends who go back a long way. ANNIE is like a second mother to the kids.

GEORGE (*off*). Come here you dirty little baster . . .

ELLA. What the bleeding hell has he done now?

GEORGE. Done? I tell you what he bloody done Mrs. He bloody make a show of me. All your family alway make a bloody show of me. Ten year I been going that mosque, now I can't look mullah in bloody face now! Because he (*Points to* SAJIT.) got bloody . . . . tickle-tackle.

    SAJIT *goes over to* ANNIE.

ANNIE. What's to do cock?

ELLA. What are you going on about you big daft get. What bleeding tickle-tackle?

GEORGE. I tell you stupy, why you no listen. Your son bloody got it . . (*He indicates his crotch.*) here tickle-tackle.

ELLA *looks over to* ANNIE, ANNIE *looks at* ELLA, *they both know something.*

MEENAH. The mullah saw it mam. He went bleeding barmy!

ELLA. Less of the bleeding you.

GEORGE (*to* MEENAH). Oi, you, who bloody asking your bloody 'pinion? What you doing looking boys in the first bloody place, don't trouble with me 'cause I bloody fix you!

ELLA. Just what did he see George?

GEORGE. Bloody everything, how he can go mosque again, when he got bloody tickle-tackle?

ELLA. Are you saying he's not been circumcised?

MEENAH. What's circumcised mam?

ELLA. You shop now!

Exit MEENAH.

GEORGE. Why you not bloody fix this thing when he was baby same as others?

ELLA. Well someone's got it wrong somewhere 'cause they were all done, all six of them.

ANNIE (*backing* ELLA *up*). I'm sure she's right George, he was in the same ward as our Clifford in Hope Hospital when he had shingles.

GEORGE (*exasperated*). Look, I know what I bloody talking about, I see you sees, mullah see, all bloody all mosque seeing. You no believe me, you bloody looking.

ELLA. Sajit come here.

SAJIT (*starts to cry*). No, you're gonna hurt me.

ELLA. I'm not gonna hurt you, I just want a little look, that's all.

SAJIT. Get stuffed!

ANNIE. Oi! – language.

ELLA. I'll stuff you in a minute you cheeky little bleeder, now get here and get 'em off!

SAJIT. I don't want to.

GEORGE. Hey baster, I bloody fix you, you talk to you mam like that. You already cause me enough bloody troubles today.

ANNIE. Come Saj, let me have a look, I've seen it all before. Go on I'll be dead quick.

SAJIT. Orrrr.

ANNIE. Come on, I've wiped your shitty arse before now.

ELLA. Let Auntie Annie have a look.

SAJIT. Alright, but you've got to be quick.

He opens his pants for her, she has a quick look.

ANNIE. He's right you know Ella, it's still there. (*To* SAJIT.) This is one little fish that got through the net.

GEORGE. You see, is your bloody fault.

ELLA. How the hell was I supposed to keep count, you could have remembered.

ANNIE. Nowt to worry about George, you can still get him done.

ELLA. I know who I'd like to get done.

ELLA *and* ANNIE *laugh.*

GEORGE. Is not bloody funny you knows, you just bloody fix. This tickle-tackle very embarrassing you see Annie. I have important arrangement to make, and I can't now see, 'cause of this. All men think I bad my son having this thing, has to be cutting.

ELLA. What arrangements?

GEORGE. You not need to know my bloody business Mrs.

SAJIT. I'm not going to the doctor!

GEORGE. You can't have this thing puther, it no belong to you, not our religion see, is very dirty. No worry about it, I buy you nice watch.

ELLA. Look cock, it's just a little operation, it'll be over in a day.

ANNIE. You won't feel a thing.

SAJIT *runs out.*

GEORGE. Come here baster . . .

ELLA. Leave it, he'll only get more upset.

ANNIE. I'll go and talk to him.

ANNIE *goes out through the kitchen to the shed, where* SAJIT *has locked himself in.*

ELLA. Why bother with all this now at his age?

GEORGE. What you talking about? You know nothing about my religion, you no bloody care your children have no God. Your son no Muslim with this thing, when he die he go straight to hell.

ELLA. He's not gonna be sent to hell, just because he's got a foreskin.

GEORGE. You see, I try to explain to you, but you no bloody listen.

ELLA *sits back and lights a fag, she's heard this lecture before.*

ELLA. I'm always bleeding listening, you never get a word in edgeways with you.

GEORGE. All your bloody children run wild, but I telling you Mrs, no more, because I'm fixing them. I bloody show them.

ELLA. You tried that with Nazir and look what happened.

GEORGE. I tell you, if I see that boy Nazir in my house, I bloody kill him baster.

ELLA. Your house? Whose frigging name's on the rent book!

GEORGE. Maybe your name Mrs, but my shop money pay bloody rent.

ELLA. Oh yeah, and what do you think I do in that chippy from eight thirty in the morning 'til twelve thirty at night, count the mushy fucking peas!

GEORGE grins slightly, these arguments happen all the time, and this one has reached its point.

GEORGE. How bloody hell I know what you do all day, every time I look, you sit with Annie, talking, smoking, smoking talking. Nobody serve bloody chips.

ELLA. We work hard in that shop, and as for being sat around well you're a fine one to talk, ever since this trouble started in Pakistan, you're never away from the telly.

GEORGE. I have to take interest you sees, family in Azad Kashmir, near bloody border. Bloody make me worry.

ELLA. The answer's no.

GEORGE. What you bloody talking about 'No' (*He grins.*) I not bloody ask anything.

ELLA. You don't need to, I can read your bleeding mind like the back of me hand, so you can piss off if you think you're bringing her over here.

GEORGE. I not understand why you talk to me like this my darling.

ELLA *smiles.*

ELLA. Never mind darling, if she steps foot in this country, I'm off, and I'll take the bleeding kids with me.

GEORGE. Why is big problem, first wife always treat second wife like sister. All live together happy.

ELLA. You think you're funny don't you? Well, she'll have nowt to be happy about if she walks in here, 'cause I'll wipe the smile right off her friggin' face!

GEORGE (*smiles*). I just joke with you, you my only wife in England.

Enter ANNIE.

ANNIE. He's locked himself in the coal shed again.

GEORGE. I tell you, this boy bloody stupy I think, no full shilling. Every time I walk in street with him, he talking to bloody self. Every time he turn corner, he bloody cutting, cutting. (*He makes a scissor cutting motion.*) Bloody mentals.

ANNIE. Has he had the coat off yet?

ELLA. No. Won't let anyone go near it, it'll have to come off soon, though, 'cause it bleeding stinks.

GEORGE. I thought bloody dog shitting in house. No, it bloody Sajit. I rip baster thing off him soon.

ANNIE. Leave it, he'll come out of it, it's just a phase. Our Clifford had one with a bit of Plasticine and a pumice stone.

GEORGE. Why he alway go hide in bloody coal shed? Kid in a Pakistan no like this.

ELLA. No, you're all so perfect over there aren't you.

GEORGE (*wags his finger at* ELLA). You not bloody start with me again Mrs or I send bloody invitation to Mrs Khan number one, in a Pakistan. I say, 'Come bloody quick, second wife give me bloody troubles.'

ELLA (*taking it in good humour*). Piss off.

GEORGE. I go butcher now, buy some chicken, you and Annie open up, I be back 'bout five.

ELLA. If you go past the shop, tell our Abdul to come and get Sajit out of the shed, we've a delivery at two and it took us half an hour to dig him out last time.

GEORGE *goes out.*

ANNIE (*checks to see* GEORGE *has gone*). You bleeding knew about Sajit didn't you?

ELLA. I did, but it had gone right out of me mind, he was supposed to be done, but the hospital cancelled it 'cause he got flu. George never found out, and what he didn't know wouldn't hurt him.

ANNIE. You knew he'd find out sooner or later you daft sod.

ELLA. Oh yeah, and when was the last time you saw George washing a baby or wiping a shitty arse? You know Saleem had such a hard time of it when he was done, I don't think I could have listened to another one of 'em screaming in pain.

ANNIE. Mm. Now you're gonna have to.

Beat.

ELLA. That bastard's up to something, I don't know what yet, but I can feel it in me bones.

ANNIE. Has he started buying material?

ELLA. Every time he comes back from the market he's got another six yards.

ANNIE. What does he do with it?

ELLA. Presents. He sends it to Pakistan for them to make clothes, then they send us Sinbad waistcoats and he puts them in the trunk in the attic. He bought some silk the other week, bloody nice stuff as well, yards of it, must have cost a bomb.

ANNIE. It don't come cheap Ella.

ELLA. He's a bastard, sends silk to her in Pakistan and I'm lucky if I can afford a bit of net curtain for the bleeding parlour!

They both laugh.

Chip shop door opens.

Act One, Scene Two

The BOYS *and* MEENAH *run into the chip shop, throwing* MANEER's *skull cap between them.* TARIQ *jumps onto the counter with it.* SALEEM *starts to mop the floor,* MEENAH *follows him round with a couple of old rags on her feet drying it off.* TARIQ *tosses the cap back to* MANEER *and stretches out on the counter.*

TARIQ. The thing is Maneer, even if your cap is religious, people round here just think you've got a tea cosy on your head.

ALL *laugh except* MANEER.

SALEEM. Where's that little twitching twat, he should be here doing this. I've got a still life that's got to be handed in by Monday.

TARIQ (*posh voice*). Oh have you Saleem, what a bleeding shame. And you've still the fish to cut and batter.

MEENAH. Me dad's going ape shit over there.

MANEER. He looked dead embarrassed in the mosque, I thought he were gonna cry.

TARIQ. Tough. Look, whatever happened with Twitch, it got us out of that place quick, and that's alright in my book.

SALEEM. You only go to the mosque once a week, you ought to try it every night, and do project work for college.

TARIQ. You sit on your arse drawing all day with felt tip pens. You don't know the meaning of hard work yet, just wait till Genghis finds out you're doing an art course, and not the engineering he thinks you're doing. I tell you mate, you'll be behind this counter servin' chips before the paint's dried on your palette.

SALEEM. Yeah, well he won't find out unless someone tells him, will he Tariq?

TARIQ. Don't look at me, it's Maneer you've got to watch, he's the one sharing hat tips with old Genghis, aren't you Gandhi?

MANEER (*he's heard the same old jokes before*). Yeah right Tariq, funny, now will you get off the counter so I can clean it.

Enter ABDUL *carrying two baskets of potatoes.*

ABDUL. Tariq, do as you're told and let him clean it. You can start chipping these spuds. (*To* SALEEM *and* MEENAH.) Haven't you two finished yet?

SALEEM. Yeah, alright Abdul, we're doing it, God you're beginning to sound just like me dad.

MEENAH. He'll be kicking our heads in, in a minute.

The OTHERS *start to laugh.*

MEENAH (*mimicking* GEORGE). 'Hey you move baster, I bloody kill you!'

ABDUL. Just get it done alright, Meenah?

TARIQ (*to* ABDUL). What time are we supposed to be going to Bradford tomorrow?

ABDUL. Poppah Sadeq's gonna pick us up at nine.

MEENAH. Are we all going?

ABDUL. No, just us two.

MANEER. But it's a first Sunday, we always all go to Bradford on a first Sunday.

ABDUL. Well not this time.

TARIQ. Ask me Dad if you can go instead of me Gandhi. Last place I want to be this weekend is Bradistan.

ABDUL. The spuds, Tariq.

TARIQ. I don't see why I should go and meet more relatives, I'm related to half of Bradford as it is.

We hear knocking at the door, TARIQ *pulls aside the net curtain on it.*

TARIQ. Me dad!!

Everyone starts to panic. SALEEM *picks up the mop and bucket and runs around the other side of the counter where he starts to batter the fish.* TARIQ *leaps over the counter and chips potatoes in the chipper at an alarming rate.* MEENAH *shuffles around maniacally trying to dry the floor, While* MANEER *wipes everything in sight.*

Enter GEORGE.

GEORGE. Abdul, go over to house, Sajit in a coal shed.

MANEER. Dad, can I go to Bradford tomorrow as well?

GEORGE. No. You coming with me to mosque here, we go to see mullah, you come as well Saleem, and you Meenah.

SALEEM. I've got some college work to do dad.

GEORGE. This more important. (*Looks at* TARIQ'*s hair.*) Why you not cutting you bloody hair when I tell you? You looking like bloody pansy. Get bloody cut.

TARIQ. Right dad.

GEORGE. Short back-a-side. (*To* SALEEM.) And why you wear this stupid clothes? Where suit I buy you in market for you wear college? I not made-a bloody money you know Mr.

The OTHERS *can barely hold in their laughter.*

SAJIT. Me mam took it to the cleaners dad.

GEORGE. You bloody lucky go to college. I come to this country with nothing. Now what I got?

MEENAH. You've got a chip shop dad.

GEORGE. I got own business see. You better chance than me see, go a college. So you sees, if you hair is tidy, and you looking smart, teacher looking see. May be help find job after. Always plenty job for engineer. Lota job in a Pakistan, do good business there. Buy house in Islamabad, very nice bungalow there.

SALEEM. Yeah, erm, long way off that though dad.

GEORGE. You never know. Life change all a time, never know what bloody happening see's. When I first come to this country, in 1930, I here one year maybe and I make bloody film.

MEENAH, TARIQ, and MANEER can barely keep a straight face. ABDUL has to get away.

MEENAH. What film was that dad?

GEORGE. Maybe is name was 'Sabu Elephant' or 'The Drum'. Alexander Korda make film or maybe he brother.

TARIQ. Were you the star dad?

GEORGE. No bloody star stupy, I shouting in crowd. 'I kill bloody English'. One day my friend say come make film, they want Indian. So I go. Mr Korda very good man, one day, we all sit down eating, and he come in with woman who play actor. She say not want to eating with these people. He say, then you bloody get lost, 'cause I wanting to eat with them. Then he send her bloody away.

MEENAH. He sounds alright him dad.

GEORGE. He very good man, look after see. Why you laughing? No many people treat like this, 'cause we Pakistani.

MEENAH. We're not laughing dad, are we?

TARIQ. No dad.

MANEER. No.

GEORGE. I very strong when I young, very fit, I use bend bars. People say you looking same as Errol Flynn! I go now, Tariq do two basket potatoes.

GEORGE *exits.*

TARIQ. Errol Flynn? More like Charlie bleeding Chaplin!

They all start to laugh.

Act One, Scene Three

It's early morning at the Khans' house, ELLA comes from the kitchen with a tray full of cups and three packets of chocolate biscuits. She sits and opens a letter and lights a fag. Enter GEORGE carrying a plastic bucket his head to one side, it's the piss bucket. ELLA *winces at the smell.* GEORGE *goes out to empty it.*

GEORGE. I bloody tell Tariq empty this. I bloody kill him, baster.

ELLA. Letter here from the doctor, said he can get Sajit into Salford Royal on Tuesday. He's got to have a check up later today. So you'll have to open up.

GEORGE. Good.

ELLA. Your tea's here, do you want biscuits or I can make you some toast?

GEORGE. Just half a cup, and biscuit. (*He exits.*)

ELLA *pours tea from one of the cups into her own. She picks up a paper and reads. Re-enter* GEORGE.

GEORGE. Any news about war in Pakistan?

ELLA. Yeah, I've just read something here 'There has been further unrest in Dacca, capital of East Pakistan, since the arrest of Sheik Mujib. West Pakistan has now declared martial law.'

GEORGE. More problem now I think, these people no good. Bloody India stir up trouble for Pakistan.

ELLA. Well they only want their democratic rights, it's not much to ask for is it.

GEORGE. They bloody ask India to come, maybe take Azad Kashmir. Kashmir belong to Pakistan, whole country Muslim see. Mountbatten and bloody Nehru fixing it baster.

ELLA. If you're going to the fish market, we need some more plaice, we ran out last night.

GEORGE. I tell you we going to lose half bloody country now.

ELLA. Only the East side. You said yourself they weren't proper Pakistanis, so I don't know what you're so bothered about. Better get some more cod as well while you're at it.

GEORGE. Of course I bloody worry, family in Azad Kashmir, on border. They'll be in danger.

She goes over to the door, opens it and shouts.

ELLA. Well you're not, so think yourself lucky. (*Shouting.*) Abdul, Tariq, Maneer, Saleem, Meenah, Sajit, get up, your breakfast's ready!

GEORGE. Mr Shah coming Sunday week for visit.

ELLA. Oh aye, I thought you didn't like him?

GEORGE. Stupy, I never say I no like him, his family live near my village, nearly like family see. He been here twenty year, got double extension.

ELLA. How many are coming?

GEORGE. Mr Shah only . . . He have two daughters you know, same age as Abdul and Tariq.

ELLA is instantly suspicious.

ELLA. Oh yeah.

GEORGE. That's why they coming here Sunday, we celebrate engagement.

ELLA. I knew you were up to something, why didn't you tell me, for that matter, why haven't you told them?

GEORGE. Why I need to tell you my bloody business. Is my decision no yours. Or bloody kid. I their bloody father, they do as I say. Anyway, we sort out on Sunday. I go now, tell Tariq do five basket potatoes.

ELLA. George, you're gonna have to say something before Sunday.

GEORGE exits. ELLA is by the door, she shouts.

Abdul, Tariq, Maneer, Saleem, Meenah, Sajit get up now!

ELLA sits down and lights a fag. Enter ABDUL. She is not sure if she should say something.

ABDUL. What time is it mam?

ELLA. Five past seven, you'd better hurry or you'll be late for work.

ABDUL. It's alright, Steve's giving us a lift on his bike.

ELLA. Oh you be careful on that thing, he's like a bloody madman on it. What time did you get in from Bradford last night?

ABDUL. 'Bout half twelve, Jehan Khan sent a load of kebabs and fruit, they're in the fridge.

ELLA. Was your dad up when you got in?

ABDUL. Yeah, is he up yet? I forgot to tell him there's a meeting in Bradford next week. He's got to phone Poppah Zahir.

ELLA. He's gone to the fish market . . . did he say owt to you?

ABDUL. Just asked about Bradford, why?

ABDUL *realises something's not right.*

ABDUL. What's he up to mam?

ELLA (*reluctant to say anything*). He's just told me he's gonna get you and Tariq engaged on Sunday week.

ABDUL. You what!

ELLA. To the Shahs' daughters.

ABDUL. Why hasn't he said owt to me? All he talked about last night was being a good Muslim and the trouble in East Pakistan!

ELLA. I don't know, perhaps he thought you might do a runner like Nazir.

ABDUL. I'm not Nazir. Why does he never trust me mam? He makes decisions about my life as if he owned it.

ELLA. He thinks he does.

ABDUL. Why didn't you say something to him!

ELLA. Abdul, what makes you think he's gonna start listening to me?

Pause.

ABDUL. I don't want to talk about this now, I'm going to work!

He storms out slamming the door.

ELLA. Abdul! I don't bleeding believe this family. (*She goes over to the door.*) Tariq, Maneer, Saleem, Meenah, Sajit, get up!

Beat.

If you're not up in five minutes, you're dead!

She sits down and lights a fag. MEENAH *enters.*

MEENAH. Morning. (*She takes a cup and biscuits.*)

ELLA. About bleeding time too.

MEENAH. You're bright and cheerful this morning, mam.

ELLA. Less of the cheek as well, gobby.

MEENAH. What's wrong with our Abdul?

ELLA (*taps her nose*). Mind that. Drink your tea and get over to the shop, the floors need mopping.

MEENAH. Can I go to the school club tonight with Judy and Mary? Mary's mam said she'd take us and bring us back?

ELLA. I don't know why you're asking, 'cause you know you're going to the mosque later.

MEENAH. Oh, mam it's not fair.

ELLA. And you can put that bleeding lip away as well lady.

MEENAH. But these Pakistani girls always get me into trouble in the van.

ELLA. Well if you stopped to think before you hit them, you'd save yourself a lot of bother. Now get your breakfast eaten and look sharp.

Enter MANEER.

MANEER. Mam, Tariq came in through the window last night and left it open.

ELLA. Was he out again last night?

MANEER. He's never in.

MEENAH. You've got a right gob on you, you.

ELLA. I'll have that bleeder when he comes down.

Enter SALEEM.

SALEEM. Mam, Sajit had his coat on again last night.

MEENAH. He's a mong him mam.

MANEER. I've got a scratch right down me back from the zip.

ELLA. Well tell him to take it off before he gets into bed.

MANEER. He won't listen to us, he just tells us to get stuffed
    and gets into bed.

ELLA. Well take it off him.

SALEEM. No way, I'm not touching him!

MEENAH. Have you felt that coat, it's all greasy, he's
    hanging.

Enter SAJIT, *takes a cup and a whole packet of biscuits.*

MEENAH. Hey, one at a time Twitch.

SAJIT. Get stuffed you.

ELLA. Sajit you've got an appointment with the doctor later
    on.

SAJIT *jumps up and runs out.*

ELLA. That boy'll be the death of me. Right, I'm going over to
    the shop. Meenah, Maneer, don't take forever over your
    breakfasts. As soon as Tariq comes down tell him to phone
    Holland's and put the pie-order in. Then come over to the
    shop and help me change the oil in the fryers. Saleem, the
    money for your model's on the mantelpiece.

She exits.

MANEER. What's Twitch got to go to the doctor's for?

SALEEM *goes to the mantelpiece to get his money.*

SALEEM. Don't know, there's a letter here

MEENAH. What's it say?

SALEEM (*reading*). Says it can get him into Salford Royal on Tuesday.

MANEER. What's all that about then?

SALEEM. Must be because he's a bit daft.

MEENAH. Daft? He's a fucking idiot, he wears a parka twenty four hours a day. He doesn't need a doctor, he wants locking up.

Enter TARIQ.

TARIQ. Who wants locking up?

MEENAH. Twitch, me mam's having him put away. And Maneer told me mam that you came in through the window last night, didn't you gob-shite?

MANEER. It was freezing cold when I got up to pray this morning.

TARIQ *goes over to* MANEER *and starts to ruffle his hair.*

TARIQ. Ohh, did Gandhi have to pray in the coldy-poldy. Ohhh, what a shame.

ELLA *has entered behind* TARIQ, *she slaps him across the head.*

TARIQ. Ouch! What was that for?

ELLA. Where the bleeding hell were you last night?

TARIQ. In bed.

ELLA. Whose bleeding bed, that's what I want to know?

TARIQ. Me own.

ELLA. That's not what I heard. From now on I want to know your every move lad. You go nowhere this week, without me or your dad knowing. Now get your tea drunk, and get over to the shop and change the frigging oil in the ovens.

TARIQ. But mam . . .

ELLA. No bleeding 'buts', you've been warned, now shift it. Where are me fags? (*She sees* SALEEM *with the letter.*)

What are you doing reading my bleeding letter? Give it here; and that's another thing, one of you make sure Sajit's here, washed and scrubbed at four o'clock for the doctor's. Use the Swarfega on him, I'm not having him looking riffy and showing me up.

MANEER. What's he going to the hospital for mam?

ELLA. He's going to be circumcised if you must know.

MANEER (*over*). You what?

ELLA. So don't go taking the mickey out of him.

ELLA *exits*.

MEENAH. Is that what the chop is then?

TARIQ. The jammy little bastard, how's he got away with that for so long. God, what I wouldn't give to have a foreskin.

MEENAH. I've never seen one.

SALEEM. We draw them all the time at college, it's nothing special.

MEENAH. What, people stand there naked and you draw them?

MANEER. Better not let me mam find out.

SALEEM. It's part of the course, dick-head.

MANEER. Doesn't sound like art to me.

SALEEM. What fucking art do you know about Gandhi?

MEENAH. Draw us a foreskin then.

SALEEM. You what?

MEENAH. Draw us a foreskin.

SALEEM. Give us that pen off the fireplace then.

SALEEM *takes some paper from his bag and begins to draw a foreskin. The others look on.*

SALEEM (*drawing*). It's that bit there, it protects the end of the penis.

MEENAH. Hey that's dead good that, Saleem, in' it Tariq?
Looks just like a real bloke. I didn't know you could draw
that good.

SALEEM. I wouldn't be on a foundation art course if I
couldn't draw Meenah, there'd be no point in it.

MEENAH. Yeah, I know, am just saying that this is the first
time I've seen you do it. God, do a Poindexter on me or
what!

MANEER. Foreskins are dirty.

TARIQ. If they're dirty, what are they doing there in the first
place?

MEENAH. What are they gonna do with it after they cut it off?

TARIQ. Make it into a kebab for him. They throw it away you
div-head.

MEENAH. What do they cut it off for?

MANEER. Because you have to.

SALEEM. It lessens the feeling on your nob.

MANEER. No it doesn't.

TARIQ. How would you know, you haven't used it yet.

SALEEM. He's been trying, he were after Katy Jones the other
day.

MEENAH. Katy Jones the bag of bones, everyone's snogged
her.

MANEER. No I wasn't.

TARIQ. What'll me dad say about that Gandhi, caught trying
to snog the bag of bones.

MEENAH. Even Twitch has snogged her.

Enter SAJIT, he goes for the biscuit packet.

MEENAH. Hey Twitch, you see this. (*Shows him the picture.*)
You're not gonna have it next week. Me dad's having your
nob cut off.

The OTHERS *laugh.*

SAJIT. Get stuffed.

MEENAH. Don't frigging start you little pleb or I'll drop you.

TARIQ. Come on, we better get over the shop. Sajit be here at four o'clock or I'll burn that coat off your back.

TARIQ, MANEER, *and* SALEEM *make to go,* SALEEM *pulls a portfolio from behind the couch where it's been hidden.* MEENAH *gives* SAJIT *a clip across the head.*

MEENAH. Four you mong. Don't forget. (*They exit.*)

SAJIT *takes the drawing, looks at it, then pulls his pants forward to compare it with his own. He looks puzzled.*

Act One, Scene Four

TARIQ *sits on the counter mopping up curry from a plate.* MEENAH *and* MANEER *are doing odd jobs around the shop, there is Indian film music playing which* MANEER *and* MEENAH *dance around to as they go about their jobs. Someone knocks at the door.* MEENAH *bops over and opens it. It's* SAJIT.

MEENAH. We said four you mong, now scram.

SAJIT. Me mam said to put some more peas on. And that I can have some mineral.

TARIQ. One bottle Twitch and that's all you're getting.

SAJIT *sees what* TARIQ's *eating.*

SAJIT. Me dad said you're not to eat the chicken curry, until the spinach is gone.

MANEER. Tariq, I told you that!

TARIQ. Oh fuck off Gandhi, since when have you been curry inspector?

SAJIT. I'm gonna tell me dad. (*He climbs on the counter.*)

TARIQ (*knows he has to pay the price*). One bottle of pop Twitch and that's all you're getting.

SAJIT. Is there any cold chips left?

MEENAH (*gives him a can and knocks him off the counter*). No there isn't.

MANEER. It's not fair Tariq, I got blamed last time.

TARIQ. Will you stop whinging. And turn that crap off, it's giving me a headache.

MANEER *doesn't do anything*, TARIQ *jumps over the counter, switches the music off and returns to his position.*

MEENAH. Oi, I was listening to that as well.

TARIQ. Tough. I hate Paki music, go and make us some chappatis.

MEENAH. Paki enough when you want feeding aren't you? Well you can fuck off if you think I'm gonna wait on you!

SAJIT. I'll make 'em if I can have some cold chips.

MEENAH *and* MANEER *laugh.*

TARIQ. Do you think I'm gonna put owt in my mouth that's been in your hands?

SAJIT. I'll wash 'em.

TARIQ (*laughing*). I don't care if you soaked them in Dettol for a week, I still wouldn't eat them.

SAJIT. Orrr, go on, I'm dead good.

TARIQ (*to* SAJIT). Come here, Shuuuut, uuuup!

TARIQ *shakes vinegar onto* SAJIT *from the bottle on the counter.* MEENAH *and* MANEER *look on laughing.*

SAJIT. Get stuffed you. (*He retreats to a corner and mopes.*)

MEENAH. So who were you with last night?

TARIQ. Wouldn't you like to know.

MEENAH. Come on, I told you that Maneer grassed on you.

TARIQ. Alright . . . it was June Higgins.

SAJIT (*from his corner*). She's a slag her!!

TARIQ. Button it Twitch, you don't even know her.

SAJIT. Yeah I do, they live down Markindale Street, her mam goes out with that bloke with the limp who comes in here every Tuesday for fish and chips twice.

MANEER. Auntie Annie said the mother was a tart, and if the daughter wasn't reined in she'd go the same way as well.

SAJIT. She'll shag owt.

MEENAH. Take no notice Tariq, he knows fuck-all.

SAJIT. I know more about what goes on in this house than you do!

MEENAH. Bollocks!

SAJIT. I know all about the engagem . . .

   MANEER *cuts him off, but it's too late, the cat's out of the bag.*

MANEER. Sajit!

TARIQ. What engagement?

   SAJIT *knows he's in trouble and bolts for the door, but is held by* MEENAH. *She and* TARIQ *pin him up against the wall.*

TARIQ. Out with it Twitch!

SAJIT. Maneer knows more about it than I do, me dad took him with him 'cause I smelt. Didn't he Maneer?

TARIQ. Well Maneer, what's been going on?

MANEER. I can't tell you, me dad'll kill me. No one's supposed to know, I'm not supposed to know.

TARIQ. Maneer!

MANEER. It might not be true.

MEENAH . Come on Maneer, we've got a right to know if it's about us.

MANEER. Alright, but you haven't got it from me if it is. Yesterday when you went to Bradford with Abdul, me and Twitch went to a meeting about East Pakistan, Mr Shah was there and he came over and started talking to me dad. Then some blokes made a joke about getting his daughters married off.

SAJIT. That's when Mr Shah said it was being arranged . Then me dad smelt me and sent me home and took Gandhi with him.

TARIQ. What happened there?

MANEER. I don't know, they were talking in Pakistani.

MEENAH . Come on Maneer, you must have picked something up?

MANEER. Look, all I could understand, was Mr Shah mentioned his daughters' names, Tariq's and Abdul's and me dad agreed to something.

MEENAH . Fucking hell!

The door bursts open, they all jump, it's AUNTIE ANNIE. *She has some white sheets under her arm.*

ANNE. Is your mam not in?

MEENAH . No Auntie Annie, she's at the house.

ANNIE. Right. What are you lot up to?

MANEER. Nothing.

TARIQ. Just doing the cleaning.

ANNIE. And butter wouldn't melt in your mouth Tariq Ali Khan. Are they picking on you Saj?

SAJIT. No Auntie Annie. (*He doesn't sound convincing.*)

ANNIE. I bleeding bet, come on with me, I'm gonna see your mam.

They exit.

TARIQ. Meenah, lock that door in case me dad comes. I knew he was up to something when he didn't come to Bradford.

MEENAH. He's a right crafty old bastard, you can't afford to let your guard down with him.

MANEER. Just wait and see.

TARIQ. You wait and frigging see!

Lights up on the living room of the house as SAJIT *and* ANNIE *enter.* ELLA *is folding washing off the lazy susan.*

ANNIE. It's only me!

ELLA. Hiya.

ANNIE. Do you want to give us a hand with old Sara Mack, they've just brought her home.

ELLA. Bleeding hell that was quick, she was only in the wash-house the other day.

ANNIE. Ella, I was stood talking to her in the dockers' club last Sunday, and now I'm laying the poor bleeder out.

ELLA. You know, there's no telling is there?

ANNIE. It were a brain clot that did it, Ethel Shorrocks was in the shop when it happened. She said she went in, said 'I'll have a quarter of rodey bacon' and before she could say owt else, she were flat on her back, dead as a door nail. Funeral's on Friday, they're having salmon.

ELLA. Least it was quick, she deserved that, after putting up with that get of a husband. Do you want a cup of tea, it's just brewed?

ANNIE. Go on, I'll have a quick one, she's not going anywhere.

ELLA. Sajit go and get us another cup from the kitchen. (*He goes.*)

ANNIE (*putting her sheets down carefully*). God forgive me for speaking ill of the dead . . . but he were an evil bastard that one, from top to bleeding toe. He knocked her about something chronic.

ELLA. Didn't you do him when he died?

ANNIE. What was left of him, he was crushed on the docks by a crate of West Indian bananas. Served him right for being a biggot I say.

ELLA. Bless her. Do you think she felt owt?

ANNIE. It was all over in seconds according to Ethel but that's Ethel Shorrocks for you.

ELLA. And she's not long for this world by the looks of her.

ANNIE. Well I laid Ethel's mother out as well, and she were no older than Ethel is now. In fact she looked better dead than Ethel does alive. Her Dad said so at the time.

ELLA. He didn't?

ANNIE. He bleeding did. Good sense of humour he had, well he'd have to with Ethel's mother, oh she was depressing Ella, you couldn't stick her for more than five minutes. A right miserable bleeder. Some say he committed suicide you know.

ELLA. No!

ANNIE. Well it must have been tablets 'cause there wasn't a mark on her, we looked. It's funny, you don't get many suicides nowadays. Time was it was every other week.

ANNIE. Remember Mad Arthur in Monmouth Street, hung himself with a pair of braces.

ELLA. Did you do him?

ANNIE. No, undertakers down Ordsall Lane had him, I didn't mind really, he'd been up there two weeks before they found him. Thing is about suicides now, Ella, is all these bleedin' pills. They take so long, someone's found you before they start to work. Next thing you know you're in Salford Royal having your stomach pumped.

ELLA. They used to go t' ship canal up by Throstle's Nest, no messing see. A bag of coal and a bit of a jump and you were gone.

ANNIE. Or gas. There were them two blokes gassed themselves in that pub on't end of Regent Road.

ELLA. That's right.

ANNIE. They call it the Gas Tavern now. They used to serve cucumber butties in the afternoons. Nice lads they were, but very fussy. Hey have you seen these?

ANNIE pulls out a pair of candlesticks from her holdall.

ELLA. They're belting them, how much?

ANNIE. Fifteen bob a pair. Knock-offs from the docks. I got four, one for each corner of the coffin, I'll use the old ones for me altar piece. It'll look nice won't it?

SAJIT. I'm going in the yard mam. (*He exits.*)

ELLA. Stay out of that shed!

ANNIE. Have you sorted him out yet?

ELLA. He's going to the doctor's later, if all's well, he gets the chop next week.

Enter GEORGE with an old barber's chair.

ELLA. You're not bringing that bleeding thing in here.

ANNIE. Where've you got that from George?

GEORGE puts it down and tries it out for comfort.

GEORGE. I buy on market, is very good, very comfortable.

ELLA. It's an old barber's chair, you daft tute – the amount of bleeding rubbish he brings in here Annie. How much did you pay for it?

GEORGE. Why you bloody complain, I buy for you my love, is no expenses, four pound, no rubbish, bloody bargain.

ELLA. You want your head feeling spending four bob on that, never mind four pound you daft sod. It's bleeding junk.

GEORGE. Oi stupy, is no junk, you think I spend-a-money buy-a-junk. You bloody daft I thinks.

ANNIE picks up her sheets and hold-all.

ANNIE. Right I'm off to sort her out, I'll see you later. Ta-raa George.

She exits.

ELLA *gives up, it's obvious the chair is here to stay.*

ELLA . Do you want some tea, it's still warm?

GEORGE. I have half a cup. Kids no in yet?

ELLA. Saleem's still at college, Sajit's in the yard, the others are at the shop.

GEORGE. Come try this, you sees for self.

GEORGE *takes* ELLA's *arm and tries to sit her in the chair,* ELLA *laughs.*

ELLA. Get off you daft bleeder, I'm trying to pour your tea.

GEORGE. Try, very comfortable.

ELLA. Will you give over!

She sits in the chair.

GEORGE. See, very nice, make you relaxing.

ELLA. Yeah, very bloody nice, now do you want your tea or what?

GEORGE. I think it good, got arms, swivel, everything.

ELLA. It'll take more than a bloody swivel to make me relax around you.

SAJIT i*s in the kitchen getting a biscuit, he listens by the door.*

GEORGE. I buying nice material in a market.

ELLA. Oh aye.

GEORGE. Send some to Pakistan, celebrate engagement, and five suits for Shah's family.

ELLA. What do they need to celebrate for in Pakistan. Haven't they got enough to worry about with this war on?

GEORGE. What you bloody talking about stupy. You not understand my mind.

ELLA. Well amongst all this buying of presents and celebration, are you gonna tell Abdul and Tariq what's going on?

GEORGE. If I want telling Abdul and Tariq, I speak when I want bloody speaking, is not your bloody business. I fixing everything see.

ELLA (*under her breath, but audible enough for* GEORGE *to hear*). Yeah, just like you fixed our Nazir.

GEORGE. I bloody hear what you saying Mrs, I no bloody daft. Why you alway mention this pucker baster name to me, how many time I tell you he dead.

ELLA. No he's not, he's living in Eccles, he might be dead to you, but he's still my son.

GEORGE. Son, he not bloody son. He should be here working in my bloody shop. Oh no, not like my shop, no like chip shop, he want be bloody hairdresser.

ELLA. He had a right to know what was happening,

GEORGE. Right, what you mean right, Pakistani believe if father ask son doing something son follow father instructions, has respect see. Nazir follow bloody pansy hairdresser instructions, but I tell you, this no happen again, 'cause I bloody teach others respecting me.

ELLA. Not by force you won't George.

GEORGE. I should have sent all bloody kids to Pakistan, when young, other wife teach bloody respect.

ELLA. Over my dead body you would have done.

GEORGE. Your bloody son bloody mad! Your daughter walking round in bloody short skirt like bloody prostitute!

ELLA. It's her school uniform! What more can the girl do to please you? The moment she finishes school she's back here and changed into trousers. She never moves off the bleeding doorstep unless I say so or she's in the shop.

GEORGE. I tell you my family in Pakistan show me bloody respect, she listen what I tell her doing.

ELLA. Alright George, bring her over here and send us over
there. Let her graft in that shop while I sit around on me arse
and wait for money to be sent over. But I'll tell you one
thing, she'll find it hard serving fish and chips wrapped up
from head to toe in a bleeding bed sheet. Hiding her beauty?
If she's that frigging beautiful, why haven't you been back
in twenty years!

*GEORGE gets up and storms out of the room slamming the
door as he goes. SAJIT runs out and goes to the shop, he'll
get there ahead of GEORGE.*

ELLA. That door'll be off its hinges by the end of the week.

*Lights up in the shop. TARIQ, MEENAH, MANEER and
SALEEM. His portfolio leans against the counter. Same
day and time.*

TARIQ. I don't fucking believe this, he can't do this to me, I'm
not gonna marry a Paki.

MEENAH. What you gonna do Tariq?

SALEEM. Now you're sure he didn't say owt about me?

MANEER. No Saleem, you weren't even mentioned.

SALEEM. So, it's just you and Abdul, Tariq.

TARIQ. There's no need to sound so pleased about it Saleem!

SALEEM. I'm not, honest, I'm just saying, you know, thank
God it's not me 'cause I'd miss out on going to university.

MEENAH. Shut it Saleem, alright.

*There's banging at the door. MEENAH looks through the
curtain.*

SAJIT. It's me dad!

MEENAH. Me dad's coming! (*She lets him in.*)

SAJIT. Quick, Genghis is coming, and he's just had an
argument with me mam.

*They all run out, MANEER grabbing what's left of
TARIQ's curry. SALEEM runs out then remembers his*

portfolio, returns and gets it. Enter GEORGE. *He's upset,
he goes over to the counter, leans against it and sobs into
his hands. He does not see* SAJIT *watching him from the
doorway.*

Act One, Scene Five

Tuesday a week later. SAJIT *is sat on a wheelchair.* GEORGE
is trying to strap a wristwatch to his wrist.

ELLA. I told you, stop playing with that.

GEORGE. You see puther, I tell you I buy you watch, is very
    special watch it tell you when to pray see, in Arabic. When
    you learn reading Arabic, you know when to pray.

   ELLA *looks at* GEORGE, *bemused.*

ELLA. The last thing he wants to be doing, is squatting down
    on his knees in his condition.

GEORGE. I know this stupy.

SAJIT. What did they cut off dad? Meenah said they'd cut me
    balls off as well.

   GEORGE *does not know what to say.*

GEORGE . You no need bloody worry about that.

ELLA. Take no notice of her.

   A DOCTOR *comes over to them.*

DOCTOR. Excuse me, it's Mr and Mrs Khan isn't it?

ELLA. Yes.

DOCTOR. I'm Doctor Krishna Mehta. Do you think I can have
    a word with you?

ELLA. Erm, of course, doctor . . . George.

GEORGE. You Indian?

DOCTOR. I'm sorry?

ELLA. Shut up George. It's nothing serious is it, doctor, I mean with our Sajit? 'Cause we'd like to know straight away.

GEORGE. Everything okay doctor? Tickle-tackle all gone?

DOCTOR. The what?

ELLA. Oh for Christ sake George, do you have to keep saying that. Sorry doctor, but he'd make a bloody saint swear.

GEORGE. What you know Mrs, what you want me to say?

DOCTOR. I think you both ought to know, that the circumcision was absolutely fine. No, it's not that I want to talk about.

ELLA. Oh.

DOCTOR. We are concerned about him though.

ELLA. He's not said anything to anyone has he, swore at you or something?

DOCTOR. No, nothing like that, I was wondering Mrs Khan, how long has he had his coat?

A beat, the penny drops.

ELLA. You've noticed that then doctor?

DOCTOR. One could hardly fail to.

ELLA. Well you know what kids are like with new fashions, they never want to take them off.

DOCTOR. Mrs Khan, it wasn't until he was under the anaesthetic that we could get it off him.

ELLA *looks at* GEORGE.

ELLA. It's the coat.

GEORGE. Well you baster buy for him, now baster never come out. You see in my country these things never happen. I been this country forty year . . .

ELLA. Aye, and you still know nowt.

GEORGE. How many time I tell you, boy bloody stupy. He
   bloody pogle doctor, this boy always bloody belkuf. You
   Indian, you know what I mean.

DOCTOR. Well I don't think he's mad, but there are a couple
   of things we'd like to look into.

ELLA. He just has his little quirks, I mean we all do.

DOCTOR. What other quirks are they?

   Almost regretting she mentioned it.

ELLA. Well I don't know if you've noticed, when he walks
   about, especially round corners.

DOCTOR. Yes! What is that?

ELLA. He cuts a piece of string attached to his back . . . it's not
   actually there, he just believes it to be, and he cuts it off as
   he goes round corners.

DOCTOR. I'm sorry, could you explain that again?

ELLA. He thinks he has a piece of string coming out of his
   back, which he has to cut with a pair of imaginary scissors,
   as he goes round corners.

DOCTOR. Anything else?

ELLA. Not really, well he did jump head first into a cast iron
   paddling pool in Rhyl, but I think he thought it was deeper.
   Either that or he was just being clever.

DOCTOR. Was he injured?

ELLA. Oh aye, back of his head were like jelly, came up as big
   as a Mills grenade.

DOCTOR. Did he see a doctor?

ELLA. Yeah, they're very good like that at Sunny Vale, they
   brought a specialist in to see him. He tested his eyes with his
   fingers and a pendulum, that sort of thing.

DOCTOR. And?

ELLA. Well, he's never been able to keep his eyes still at the
   best of times, he's got a bit of a twitch if you've noticed.

DOCTOR. Would you mind if I asked Sajit if he'd like to come back and see me again, Mrs Khan?

ELLA. If you think it'll help, doctor.

DOCTOR. What about you Mr Khan?

GEORGE. No problem with that.

DOCTOR. Well, if you don't mind waiting here, I'll just go and have a little chat with him before you go.

The DOCTOR *goes over to* SAJIT .

GEORGE. You know he bloody Indian doctor?

ELLA. Well he's hardly likely to blame Sajit for the partition of India is he, you daft tute.

GEORGE. I not bloody trust these peoples.

ELLA. He's a bleeding doctor, not some Indian spy.

Lights up on SAJIT *and the* DOCTOR.

DOCTOR. Nearly ready to go Sajit?

SAJIT. Yeah.

DOCTOR. Sajit, we were wondering if you would like to come back and see us again.

SAJIT (*worried*). Are you gonna cut more off?

DOCTOR. No, no, just to talk.

SAJIT. What about?

DOCTOR. Anything you want to talk about, school, your family, anything.

SAJIT. Are you Pakistani?

DOCTOR . No, my family's from India, why?

SAJIT. You talk different. I know about East Pakistan.

DOCTOR. Then we can talk about that if you like.

SAJIT. Me dad says there's gonna be a war with India, and they're gonna nick the rest of Kashmir. Are you gonna do that?

DOCTOR. I'm not going to do anything, I live here and I'm a doctor, not a politician. Besides, there are ways other than war to get what you want.

SAJIT *thinks.*

SAJIT. Me and me brothers hope the Indians win, 'cept we don't want them to take Azad Kashmir, 'cause that's Pakistan's, but they can win other things, 'cause me dad'll be dead pissed off.

The DOCTOR *smiles.*

DOCTOR. Do you like it when he gets angry?

SAJIT. Me brothers do, I'm not bothered.

He beckons to ELLA *and* GEORGE. *They come over.*

DOCTOR. What are you gonna do when you get home, go out and play with your friends?

SAJIT. I can't do that, I've just had an operation.

DOCTOR. I mean after, do you play football?

SAJIT. Naa, it's boring that. I sit in our coal shed, it's dead quiet.

ELLA *has come over, followed by* GEORGE.

DOCTOR. Sajit tells me you have a coal shed, Mrs Khan.

ELLA. Yes, I feel like locking meself in there sometimes, get away from this silly bugger. (*Nod of the head towards* GEORGE. *then to* SAJIT.) I told you, stop playing with that, you'll break it and someone else has got to use it.

DOCTOR. It doesn't matter Mrs Khan.

ELLA. Does to me doctor, I'm not having my kids being accused of bad manners. People are a lot quicker to point the finger if they see they're a bit foreign. Well, not with mine. George, go order a taxi.

GEORGE *goes off.*

DOCTOR. Well, Sajit's agreed to come back and visit us, haven't you Sajit?

SAJIT. Yeah . . . I sunbathe on the shed as well, I don't always sit in it. I'm not mad you know.

DOCTOR. Do you wear your coat when you sunbathe?

SAJIT. Yeah, and sun-glasses.

DOCTOR. Tell me about cutting the string when you go round corners?

SAJIT. That? I don't do that any more.

GEORGE *comes back, takes* SAJIT's *bag.*

GEORGE . Ella, taxi become downstairs.

DOCTOR. Well, that's very good Sajit, 'cause when we get together and . . .

SAJIT. I use an axe now, 'cause the string's turned to rope.

End of Act One.

Interval.

Act Two, Scene One

MEENAH *and* TARIQ *are sat with a plate of bacon and sausages between them. MEENAH gets up and sprays air freshener around. SALEEM tries to cover the food.*

TARIQ. 'Kinell, Meenah, watch what you're doing!

MEENAH. It stinks of burnt bacon in here, me dad'll smell it a mile off.

TARIQ. Chuck some curry powder about, that'll cover it.

She goes into the kitchen and comes out sprinkling curry powder around.

TARIQ. How long's me mam been at the hospital?

MEENAH. 'Bout an hour, we got plenty of time. Where's Saleem, not like him to miss a fry up?

TARIQ. Said he'd be late, something to do with his model, said to save him some though.

MEENAH. He can piss off, he should be taking the risk if he wants to eat. 'Kin college boy. Me mam's mad, she keeps buying him felt tip pens from the market. He's got 'em all piled up upstairs. Even Auntie Annie gets them for him now, he'll be able to open a shop soon.

TARIQ. See that dressing gown me dad bought for Sajit, just because he's getting the chop?

MEENAH (*cynically*). Yeah right, it'll look great under his parka, you spoke to our Abdul yet?

TARIQ. I tried to, but he won't say owt.

We hear a knock on the door, they both freeze.

MEENAH. Who is that?

She goes into the parlour, TARIQ *picks up the plate of food ready to run.*

MEENAH (*off*). It's alright, it's only Saleem.

She goes out of the parlour to let him in. they both come into the living-room, SALEEM *carrying his portfolio.*

SALEEM. I hope you saved me some of that?

He grabs some sausage and bacon.

MEENAH. Alright Saleem, it's not leaving the frigging country, 'kinell, he's like a bleedin' gannet. (*She mimics* SALEEM *grabbing the food.*)

TARIQ *and* MEENAH *laugh.*

SALEEM. Oh cool it Meenah, you're a drag.

MEENAH *and* TARIQ *laugh at this.*

MEENAH (*taking the mickey*). Yeah, right, Saleem, I'll cool it, hey yeah. Let's go to college. Cool it! Who the fuck do you think you are?

Suddenly the door opens behind them. They all scream at the prospect of it being GEORGE, *but it is only* MANEER.

MEENAH. Ahhh!

SALEEM. Ahhh!

TARIQ. Ahhh!

MANEER. I can smell that from outside!

TARIQ. Where did you get a front door key from Gandhi?

MANEER. Off me dad.

TARIQ. Can you believe that, old enough to get married to some bird who dresses like Sinbad the sailor, with a hole through her nose, and he gives Gandhi his own key.

MEENAH. What a twat!

MANEER. Yours is called Nigget, not Sinbad.

TARIQ. Nigget! Bleeding Nigget! What sort of a come on is that? Nigget my lovely, shed those silken pantaloons and lay your head on my palliasse.

SALEEM. Thought about what you're gonna do, Tariq?

TARIQ. Not marrying Nigget, put it that way!

SALEEM. You've no choice really.

TARIQ. Oh shut up Saleem!

SALEEM. I'm only stating facts.

MANEER. What's Abdul said about it?

TARIQ. Oh he's fucking useless.

SALEEM. I still think you've no choice.

TARIQ. I have. I either stay here and have me dad tell me what to do for the rest of me life, or I do what our Nazir did and go.

MEENAH. You can't do that Tariq, what about me mam?

MANEER. She's right, me mam got a right bollocking when Nazir left.

SALEEM. You can't let her go through that again.

TARIQ. Yeah, alright, I know what happened, but I think she got bollocked 'cause he wanted to be a hairdresser, not 'cause he didn't get married.

We hear banging on the door.

MEENAH. Who the fuck's that now?

TARIQ. Go and see, Meenah.

MEENAH. No way, I went last time.

MANEER. If me dad finds me here, he'll kill me.

TARIQ. He'll do the lot of us if he sees what we're eating.

We hear GEORGE shout through the letter box.

GEORGE. Open door!

SALEEM. Oh shit!

GEORGE. Open bloody door!

MEENAH *grabs the air freshener and starts to spray round the room, while* SALEEM, TARIQ *and* MANEER *hide the food. they run, leaving* MANEER *alone. He goes to let* GEORGE *in. suddenly* SALEEM *sprints in and grabs his portfolio and sprints out again.* ELLA *enters the parlour with* SAJIT. *She lays him on on the couch, which has been made up into a bed.* GEORGE *is there as well.* MANEER *is now in the sitting room. He checks for any evidence and sees a sausage on the floor. He picks it up, doesn't know what to do with it.*

GEORGE. I go watch the news. You want tea?

ELLA. Yeah go on then.

GEORGE *enters the living room.*

GEORGE. What you doing?

MANEER *has now thrown the sausage under the couch.*

MANEER. Just looking for my other shoes, dad.

GEORGE. What time Abdul get back from work?

MANEER. About half past five dad. How's Sajit?

GEORGE. He fine now. Put kettle on for your mam, make tea.

MANEER *goes into the kitchen.*

GEORGE. You go to mosque today puther?

MANEER (*off*). Erm, no dad, tomorrow.

GEORGE (*lights fag*). You good boy, God will help you, if you live your life believing in God. People who no follow the rules of God, he sending bloody hell. They have no chance in the world, like man we see on Sunday, he say, God say, send money, he bloody stupy, I tell you son. (*He clears his throat.*) He have nothing because he no understand God. Not educated you see. He say there is no God, we all God. This man bloody pagan . . . bhenchoud badahmarsh, if they no God, what we all bloody doing?

MANEER *is completely confused in the kitchen.*

MANEER. Yeah dad.

GEORGE. You see puther, this country not like our peoples, I been here since 1930, I try to make good life for my family. Your mother is good woman, but she not understand, son. I love my family, but all time I have trouble with people, they not like I marry you mother. Always calling you mother bad name. That why I always try to show Pakistani way to live is good way, parent look after children, children look after parent. English people not like this. All my family love each other. Bradford, Pakistan. All same, nobody different.

MANEER. I know what you're trying to say dad! (*To himself.*) It's the others you've got to convince.

Fade out in the living room and kitchen and up in the parlour.

ELLA sits next to SAJIT on the couch, he's dropped off to sleep. She hums to him and strokes his hair. ANNIE pops her head round the door. ELLA beckons her in, she's got a bag of fruit and some comics for him.

ANNIE. How's he doing?

ELLA. Alright, just a bit sore.

ANNIE. Poor little bleeder, where's old bothered balls, he happy now?

ELLA. Next door. He bought him a new dressing gown and a watch.

ANNIE. Not much of a swap, but it's better than nowt I suppose.

Pause.

ELLA. Annie . . . Do you think I'm a good mother?

ANNIE. What sort of bleeding question's that. Course you are. What's put that in your head?

ELLA. Well would you have put one of your lads through this?

ANNIE *doesn't answer.*

ANNIE. You had no choice.

ELLA. I did though Annie, I should have put me foot down and said no.

ANNIE. And given yourself a load of bleeding grief, you know what he's like.

ELLA. I know, but now he wants to marry Abdul and Tariq off. Am I to just stand by and let him throw them out when they say no?

Pause.

ANNIE. Have they said owt to you?

ELLA. Abdul won't talk about it, I think they blame me for not sticking up for them. I only found out meself the other day.

ANNIE. They're big enough and daft enough to look after themselves, Ella, you've warned them and that's all you can do, you've four more to think about. If they want to leave it's their choice. You put your foot down when it comes to Meenah, that's where you make your stand and you know it.

ELLA. Meenah? I don't think even George would tackle her.

They laugh.

ANNIE. You're a good mother to tnose kids and a bloody good wife to him as well, but you're in the middle Ella, you have to keep your head down.

Fade out.

Act Two, Scene Two

MEENAH, SALEEM, MANEER *are sat on a canal bank.*
SAJIT *charges past now and again, pushing an old pram.*
TARIQ *throws stones into the canal,* SALEEM *draws*
MEENAH.

SALEEM. Meenah, will you keep still.

MEENAH. 'Kinell Saleem, how long you gonna take, it only took you five minutes to draw a nob and a foreskin last week.

SALEEM. You can't rush an artist. (*Enter* SAJIT.)

MEENAH. Will you look at that freak!

MANEER. Oi, Twitch! Get home.

TARIQ. He moves quick for someone who's just been circumcised. Me dad say owt to you yesterday Gand?

MANEER. No, just talked about 'Songs of Praise'.

MEENAH. Yeah I bet.

MANEER. Shut it Meenah.

TARIQ. You wouldn't tell us if that Paki said owt anyway.

MANEER. You don't have to call him that Tariq.

TARIQ. It's what he is in' it?

MANEER. What does that make you?

TARIQ (*dismissively*). Oh fuck off Maneer.

MANEER. No, I won't. I've seen you with your friends taking the piss out of him on the road behind his back and it's not right, and it's not fair, (*He starts to get a bit upset.*) 'cause it's me dad you bastard! They're not your friends, they're just laughing at the stupid half-caste laughing at his own dad . . .

TARIQ. Oh stop whinging you soft twat.

SALEEM. I thought we were Anglo-Indian.

MEENAH. We're Eurasian.

SALEEM. Sound's more romantic than Paki I suppose.

TARIQ (*pointedly at* MANEER). We're English!

MANEER. We're not Anglo-Indian, not Eurasian and not English.

TARIQ. Look Maneer, if you want to be Pakistani go live in Bradford, and take me dad with you.

SALEEM *and* MEENAH *laugh.*

MANEER. No one round here thinks we're English, we're the Paki family who run the chippy, and as for our religion . . .

TARIQ. And you're well in with me dad on that one aren't you?

MANEER. It's my choice, I like it, I wouldn't force it on anyone, I don't think me dad should either. He's wrong to do that. But being Pakistani is more than just a religion, Tariq, you hate me dad too much to see it.

TARIQ *says nothing.* MANEER *walks off. Fade out on them; fade in on* ABDUL *and* SAJIT *as they enter stage right.* ABDUL *has his work bag slung over his shoulder.*

ABDUL. What are you doing out here on your own?

SAJIT. The others are over there. Have you got any cold coffee left in your thermos, Abdul?

ABDUL. No, what are you doing down here on your own?

SAJIT. Hey, you're gonna get married, aren't you?

ABDUL. Who told you that?

SAJIT. I heard. So's Tariq, but he said he isn't gonna marry a Paki.

ABDUL. Did he? Well, take no notice of him, and don't call people Pakis, it's not nice.

SAJIT. Have you seen me new watch? (*He shows* ABDUL.)

ABDUL. It's a belter that Saj.

SAJIT. It's got Arabic writing in it. You can have it if you want.

ABDUL. Me dad bought it for you, why'd you not want it?

SAJIT. I can't tell the time, and I don't understand Arabic.

ABDUL *laughs and* SAJIT *joins in.*

ABDUL. What you bleeding like hey? I can teach you to do both if you like.

SAJIT. You teach me to tell the time, but not Arabic.

ABDUL laughs again, grabs SAJIT and picks him up.

SAJIT. Ahh, get off Abdul.

ABDUL (*smells his hands*). Hey Saj, in'it about time you got that parka washed?

SAJIT. Me mam keeps on shouting at me 'cause of it.

ABDUL. Why'd you keep it on?

SAJIT. I like it.

ABDUL. I like chappatis, but I don't eat them 24 hours a day.

SAJIT. This is different.

ABDUL. Why?

SAJIT (*his mood changing*). It doesn't matter.

ABDUL. Go on Saj, tell us.

SAJIT. 'Cause . . . when it's all done up . . . I'm not there . . . I don't have to listen to anyone arguing and shouting at me . . . Is that mad Abdul?

Beat.

ABDUL. Naa, Saj, it's not mad.

Fade out, and fade up on TARIQ who comes over to meet them.

TARIQ. Get lost Twitch!

SAJIT. Get stuffed!

ABDUL. Go on up to the others Saj, I'll see you in a minute . . . go on.

SAJIT runs off.

TARIQ. I spoke to our Nazir on the phone, he said if me dad chucked us out we could stay with him.

ABDUL. I don't want to live anywhere else.

TARIQ. Alright, so we both stay here and say no. If we stick together he can't do anything.

ABDUL. There's no point Tariq, he can do anything he wants.

TARIQ. What do you mean no point, you can't just sit back and let this happen!

ABDUL. I'm not like you Tariq, I've never gone against him.

TARIQ. You mean you've let him walk all over you.

ABDUL. No, I haven't.

TARIQ. Oh come on, Abdul, I've been there remember. I swore then he'd never treat me the way he treats you.

ABDUL. There were times I could have said something, Tariq, but I didn't.

TARIQ. Why didn't you!

ABDUL. You wouldn't understand.

TARIQ. Try me.

ABDUL. Because . . . I want . . . I want him to treat me like a proper son, I want him to trust me. I don't want to feel as if I'm some investment for his future.

TARIQ. Oh come on Abdul, he's never gonna give a shit about how you feel or what you think. 'I am your father, you are my son, you do as I say, bass.' That's not fucking trust.

ABDUL. I don't know . . .

TARIQ. You've been told what to do all your life, all that respect crap, it's just brainwashing. Nazir got away from it, so can you.

Pause.

ABDUL. Alright, I'll see what I can do, but you'd better pack your bags 'cause as soon as we say anything we'll be out.

TARIQ. Nice one Abdul, welcome to the West.

TARIQ *makes to go.*

ABDUL (*to himself*). I wish I had a parka.

TARIQ. You what?

ABDUL. Nothing, let's go.

Fade up on the living room. ANNIE *and* ELLA *sit listening to the radio, drinking tea and smoking.*

RADIO. 'There have been further reports of the indiscriminate destruction of buildings and summary executions by the West Pakistani army in Dacca, capital of East Pakistan. Eye witness accounts claim the university had been attacked, and many students killed. In India a statement has been issued condemning the attacks, and has called for negotiations to take place. The Indian army has been put on full alert all along the border.'

ANNIE. Well, they're up shit creek without a paddle now.

ELLA. Try telling George that they're fighting a losing battle, and will he listen? Will he bugger. It's that army lot I blame. Black-shirts the lot of them. Once they took over it all went up the spout.

ANNIE. We had a black-shirt, lived next door but one to us during the war. Tried to get the dockers out on strike, no one listened to him mind, except Billy Thomas, and that was only 'cause his dad told him his grandad was killed by a fuzzy wuzzy at Omdurman. Me mam used to hang a paraffin lamp on his back door in the air raids hoping the Germans would bomb him. He kept his bleeding head down on V.E. Day though, and he got no bunting round his door either.

ELLA. He's getting on me nerves with this war, we were in Bradford the other week, he tried to get the kids to sing the Pakistani anthem. I said they don't speak Urdu, he said tell 'em to hum.

ANNIE. You got rid of that barber's chair I see.

ELLA. It's in the shop. Hey, you remember Sabu, don't you?

ANNIE. Which one was he?

ELLA. The one George used to call Blackie . . . he had a little black moustache, made him look like Fernando Rey.

ANNIE *thinks.*

ANNIE. Oh I remember, he had hazel eyes, always laughing. What about him.

ELLA. Dead. Killed with his wife on the Snake Pass coming back from Bradford. Not a mark on 'em.

Enter GEORGE.

ANNIE. Hiya George.

ELLA. Do you want some tea?

GEORGE. I have half a cup.

ELLA *pours* GEORGE *some tea.*

GEORGE. Any news 'bout war?

ANNIE. You just missed it George, the Indians are moving troops up to the border.

GEORGE. These baster, I tell you they want do this. No help East Pakistan, wanting bloody Azad Kashmir.

ANNIE. Do your family live near the border George?

GEORGE. Near to see.

ELLA. West Pakistan should pull out George and you know it.

GEORGE (*frustrated*). Oh stupy, listen what I tell you, India only interested in Azad Kashmir.

ELLA. What about all those people they have killed in the East? (*To* ANNIE.) They had it on telly last night Annie, it was disgusting what they'd done to them.

ANNIE. Well, I'm off, he'll be home from work soon wanting to know where his tea is.

GEORGE. You good wife cook dinner for husband.

ANNIE. Well he's only getting fish fingers and a tin of beans. I'll see you in the shop after. Taraa.

She exits.

GEORGE. What you talking 'bout?

ELLA. What do you mean?

GEORGE. Why you telling people Pakistani do disgusting thing?

ELLA (*bemused*). They were last night, I don't have to tell anyone, they can see it for themselves on the news.

GEORGE. You don't know what you see, could be criminals.

ELLA. They looked like ordinary people to me, except they were chained up, holding Korans, and being hit with machetes. Now to me, I find that disgusting.

GEORGE. These bad people, want breaking country, they bloody traitors.

ELLA. I thought you were all supposed to be brothers, isn't that what Islam teaches you? And these people were murdered with Korans in their hands.

GEORGE (*getting angry*). You not wanting to understand.

ELLA. You're bloody right I don't understand, I don't want to when they behave like that.

GEORGE. I your bloody husband, you supposed to be Muslim. You should agree with me.

ELLA. Yeah, right, I'm a Muslim wife when it suits you. I'll stop being a Muslim wife at 5:30 when the shop wants opening, or one of your relatives wants help at the Home Office. Don't make me bleeding laugh George.

GEORGE. I tell you Mrs, don't starting 'cause I fix you like I fix your baster kids, you all pucking trouble with me.

ELLA. They're only trouble 'cause you don't listen to them, you never have.

GEORGE. I no have to listen, I their father.

ELLA. George, you've got to understand, things aren't like they were when you were young. Kids are different today, our kids are different, they're bleeding half-caste for a start.

GEORGE. This make no difference.

ELLA. Oh it does George, you've been stricter with them than your own family have been with theirs.

GEORGE (*very angry*). You never understand how I try to teach my children! Every time I tell you, you no listen, you married to me 25 year and know nothing. You no like my family, no respecting me, just like your baster children!

ELLA (*full stride*). I'll tell you why I don't like your frigging family, 'cause they're a bunch of money grabbing bastards, they only come round here when they want money, or when money wants sending to Pakistan, to buy more bleeding land we're not gonna live on. And do you think any of my kids are gonna get a look in, if owt happened to you?

GEORGE (*standing*). You don't talk to me like this!

SAJIT *watches them from the back window.*

ELLA. No, you haven't got an answer for that have you? Yes, 25 years I've been married to you, George, I've sweated me guts out in your bastard shop, and given you seven kids as well, and I'll tell you this for nothing, I'm not gonna stand by and let you crush them one by one because of your pig bloody ignorance.

GEORGE *grabs* ELLA *violently by her hair and pulls her to the ground. He kicks and beats her. We see* SAJIT *crying in the yard.*

GEORGE. You baster bitch! You call me pig, you pucker, you talk to me like this again I bloody kill you bitch, and burn all your baster family when you sleep!

GEORGE *storms out leaving* ELLA *crying.* SAJIT *watches* ELLA.

Act Two, Scene Three

The KHANS' *house.* TARIQ, MANEER, *and* MEENAH *are sat watching the TV.* ELLA *comes in buttoning her apron for the shop. She sits down and starts to read the paper.*

ELLA. Meenah, put the kettle on cock, I'll have a cup of tea before I go to the shop.

TARIQ. And me.

MANEER. Me too.

SAJIT. And me.

MEENAH. Don't even think about it Twitch, I'm only brewing it, Maneer can pour.

MANEER. Oh mam, I did it last time, tell Tariq to do it.

SAJIT. Yeah, let Tariq do it.

TARIQ. Button it spaz.

ELLA. You can all shut it, Gand – erm Maneer, you can pour, Tariq get some coal.

TARIQ. Touch wood I want me chair back.

He goes.

MEENAH. Mam do we all have to stay in on Sunday?

ELLA. Yeah you do, your dad said to wear that sari your Auntie Riffat brought you from Pakistan.

MEENAH. I look stupid in it.

ELLA. Don't be daft you look fine.

MEENAH. Can't I just wear me jeans instead?

ELLA.. No you can't.

MEENAH. Well I'm not putting that stud in me nose, it makes me go cross-eyed.

ELLA. Alright, but make sure your head stays covered, and Sajit I don't want to see you in that bleeding parka, d'y'hear me lad. If your dad sees you in it, he'll wipe the floor with you.

SAJIT *bolts out of the room almost knocking* TARIQ *over.*

TARIQ. What's wrong with him?

MEENAH. Nothing decapitation couldn't fix. Maneer, the kettle's boiled.

Enter SALEEM.

SALEEM. Hiya!

ELLA. Hiya cock, just finished college? Hurry up with that tea Maneer, and make Saleem one as well.

MEENAH *and* TARIQ *exchange looks at this obvious favouritism,* MEENAH *makes a wanking gesture.*

SALEEM. Mam I need another two and six for me model.

ELLA *gets her purse out and gives him the money.*

ELLA. I've got you some new felt tips as well.

TARIQ. When are we gonna see this great work of art.

SALEEM. Sunday, when it's finished, it just needs the hair putting on it.

ELLA. Don't forget we've got visitors on Sunday, so make sure you're not late.

TARIQ. How can we forget that.

MANEER *gives* ELLA *her tea.*

ELLA. Bleeding hell Maneer, what've you put in this, it tastes like piss.

MANEER. I'll make another one.

ELLA. Never mind I'm going t' shop.

She exits.

MEENAH. Sajit said me dad had a go at me mam the other day.

TARIQ. What do you want me to do about it?

MANEER. You can unpack that bag you've got upstairs for a start.

TARIQ. I've told you to mind your own fucking business Gandhi!

MEENAH. What about me mam Tariq?

TARIQ. Look, it's just in case me dad throws us out, which he will do as soon as we tell him we're not gonna get married.

MANEER. Just try to talk to him.

SALEEM. He's right, at least try.

TARIQ. What's the use, you know what he's like!

SALEEM. Let me try and talk to him.

TARIQ. Yeah sure, that'll make all the difference.

SAJIT *runs in.*

SAJIT. Me dad's coming, he said to put the news on, something's happened in Pakistan.

TARIQ. This might not be a good time.

SALEEM. There never will be Tariq.

MEENAH. Let him try Tariq, he'll be able to put it differently, and not just start shouting.

TARIQ. Yeah but . . .

MEENAH. Shut it Tariq, and get in the kitchen, Maneer, Sajit . . . Kitchen now!

They all hide in the kitchen, leaving SALEEM *on his own. Enter* GEORGE.

GEORGE. News on yet?

SALEEM. Not yet. I think they're still fighting though.

GEORGE. We not win this war I think, India bloody clever see.

SALEEM. Dad, can I talk to you?

GEORGE. All world 'gainst Pakistan see.

SALEEM. It's about Abdul and Tariq. You know dad, I don't think they think it's the right time to get married.

GEORGE (*irritated*). What you talking about 'No right time'.

SALEEM. I don't know about Abdul, but Tariq's not much older than me, he doesn't know what he wants to do with his life yet.

We can see the OTHERS *wince in the kitchen.*

GEORGE. Is not your business what I talk to Abdul and Tariq 'bout. Who bloody hell you think you are? You maybe go college, but you no bloody tell me what I doing. Understand?

SALEEM. No, dad I don't, I don't think you do either, it's not just them two, we're all fed up of being told what to do and where to go.

GEORGE. I warning you Mr! You no talking to me like this, I your father, you treating me with respect. I not bringing you up talking me like this. Pakistani son alway show respect.

SALEEM. I'm not Pakistani, I was born here, I speak English, not Urdu.

SAJIT *bolts out of the kitchen.*

GEORGE. Son, you not understand 'cause you not listen to me. I try to show you how a good way to live. You no English, English people no accepting you. In Islam, everyone equal see, no black man, or white man. Only Muslim, it special community.

SALEEM. I'm not saying it's not, I just think I've got a right to choose for myself.

GEORGE. You want choose like Nazir, han? Lose everything, go with bloody English girl? They not good, go with other men, drink alcohol, no look after.

SALEEM. Well if Pakistani women are so great, why did you marry me mam?

SALEEM *has hit a raw nerve.* GEORGE *grabs him, and pushes him on the ground and kicks and slaps him.*

GEORGE. You baster, I tell you no go too far with me, you think you bloody clever han? Pucker! You next time die baster!

He exits leaving SALEEM *crying on the floor, the* OTHERS *burst in.*

MEENAH. Are you alright Saleem?

SALEEM. He beat me up! The bastard beat me up. I won't ever forgive him for that, not ever. I hope he fucking well dies.

TARIQ (*turns to* MANEER). Well, if that's got owt to do with being Pakistani, you can stick it.

Act Two, Scene Four

Fade up on GEORGE *as he is finishing his prayers in the parlour, there is something poetic and gentle in the movements. He does not notice* ABDUL *who is standing by the door. ABDUL is visibly upset, he moves into the room, sits and watches* GEORGE. GEORGE *completes his prayers, turns and sees* ABDUL.

GEORGE. What wrong puther?

ABDUL *sobs into his hands.*

GEORGE. Son what wrong with you?

He puts his hand on ABDUL'*s head,* ABDUL *falls against* GEORGE *in a kind of embrace.* GEORGE *strokes* ABDUL'*s head. Fade out and fade in on* ABDUL *sat in the same chair alone listening to some Indian music. Enter* TARIQ.

TARIQ. Where've you been? Steve said you left work hours ago.

ABDUL. I went to the pub.

TARIQ. You don't drink.

ABDUL. It was gonna be my first act of defiance, me dad's right, it does make you sick, but not physically.

TARIQ. You're pissed. Look, it's obvious me dad's not gonna take any notice of us. So we should just go.

ABDUL. Go, and do what, live with Nazir, what happens then? I don't want to live without a family.

TARIQ. Look, you're just feeling bad about Saleem, it wasn't our fault, even Saleem said that. That's been brewing for months.

ABDUL. How can I not feel responsible for him, or me mam for that matter. I suppose you heard about that?

TARIQ. We heard he had a go at her.

ABDUL. He gave her a fucking good hiding, Auntie Annie came into work and told me, 'cause she knew me mam wouldn't. So yes I do feel responsible. Tariq. You know it doesn't even bother me about getting married, I just wanted to be consulted.

TARIQ. You've changed your tune, I thought you were gonna tell me dad where to get off?

ABDUL. You're not listening are . . .

TARIQ. Shut up Abdul you're pathetic!

ABDUL. No! you shut up Tariq! You're right, I was pathetic, tonight in the pub with the lads. We were sat drinking, telling jokes, playing music, telling more jokes. Jokes about sex, thick Irish men, wog jokes, chink jokes, Paki jokes. And the biggest joke was me, 'cause I was laughing the hardest. And they laughed at me because I was laughing. It seemed as if the whole pub was laughing at me, one giant grinning mouth. I just sat there and watched them, and I didn't belong, I was crying, crying so hard I couldn't catch my breath, so I ran and kept on running. When I got home, me dad was here praying, I watched him Tariq, and it was right, to be here, to be a part of this place, to belong to something. It's what I want. I know me dad'll always be a problem, but I can handle that now, perhaps I might make him change; but I don't want that out there, it's not who I am, it's as alien to me as me dad's world is to you.

Pause. We can just hear the music playing in the background.

TARIQ. I suppose that's it then?

ABDUL. He might be satisfied with just one of us getting married. Will you still leave?

TARIQ. I don't want anyone hurt anymore . . . I'll think of something.

He goes but pauses at the door.

TARIQ. Abdul.

ABDUL. Yeah?

TARIQ. I do understand you know . . . more than you think.

Act Two, Scene Five

The Khans' house, Sunday. ELLA is plaiting MEENAH's hair. SAJIT sits oblivious to all the confusion around him, reading a comic.

MEENAH. Ouch! Mam, you're pulling me hair out.

ELLA. Keep it bloody still then. Sajit – go upstairs and ask your Dad to give you the nit comb.

SAJIT. I 'aven't got nits.

ELLA. Well stop scratching your bleeding head. (*To* MANEER.) Are you out of that bath yet Maneer?

MANEER. I've not been in yet.

ELLA. Well, don't bother, you haven't got time. Just have a quick wash.

MANEER. Oh mam I want a bath.

ELLA. Alright. In and out quick. (*To* MEENAH.) Did you use the big pan for the curry like I told you?

MEENAH. Yeah, and I got some more chappati flour mam as well. Will you tell Maneer to help with the chappatis mam?

SAJIT. I can make chappatis mam.

ELLA. You don't go near that flour with those hands.

SAJIT. Why can't I?

MEENAH. 'Cos we'll all end up with scabs you mong!

Enter TARIQ *and* ABDUL.

TARIQ. Mam – I can't do this tie.

ELLA. Hang on, I haven't got two pairs of hands. Abdul! Fix
Tariq's tie. (*Pause.*) Where's Saleem?

TARIQ. He said he was gonna pick his model up. Mam, this
ties not right.

ELLA. Come here. (*She does* TARIQ's *tie.*) There, that'll do.
(*She strokes his hair,* MEENAH *and* ABDUL *exchange
looks.*) Go on get lost.

ELLA. Sajit go upstairs and ask your dad to get me jewellery
out of the safe. (*As* SAJIT *goes.*) And take that bleeding
parka off! Abdul, get the posh cups out of the cabinet in the
kitchen.

MEENAH. I don't know why they can't have mugs like
everyone else, they only slurp it out of the saucers.

ELLA. Well if he does don't look, I'm not having you lot
laughing and showing me up. Right, Meenah veil on! Tariq,
Abdul, let's have a look at you, you'll do. Maneer!

MANEER *appears from the kitchen,* ELLA *looks at him.*

ELLA. Brylcreem!

MEENAH. I feel stupid in this.

SAJIT *enters.*

SAJIT. You look it.

MEENAH. Shut your gob, or I'll shut it for you.

ELLA. If I catch you fighting in that sari, I'll wipe the floor
with both of you. Now go and get me some fags from
Butterworths.

MEENAH. No way, I'm not going out dressed like this.

ELLA. Sajit go and get me twenty Park Drive. Maneer, have you emptied that bath out?

MANEER. Yeah, can you get zinc poisoning from it mam?

ELLA. Don't be so bleeding stupid.

MEENAH. I wish we had a proper one, that one don't half scratch your arse.

MEENAH *gets a clip round the ear from* ELLA.

ELLA. Hey, gob-shite, I've told you once, keep it shut. We've got visitors.

SAJIT *bursts in.*

SAJIT. Mam, quick, the Paki's here!

ELLA. Oh for Jesus sake. Abdul, muzzle him will you.

ABDUL. Sajit, get over here!

MR SHAH *enters greeted by* ELLA. ELLA *leads him into the parlour, followed by the* OTHERS, SAJIT *bringing up the rear trying to see.* ELLA *has now got her slightly posh voice on.* MR SHAH *has with him two large photographs, in ornate frames, of his daughters.*

GEORGE (*off*). Ella, this is Mr Shah.

MR SHAH. Asalaam-a-lekum.

ELLA. Walekum-a-salaam. Would you like to come through to the parlour Mr Shah?

MEENAH (*to* TARIQ). What's she talking like that for?

GEORGE *introduces the boys to* MR SHAH.

GEORGE. This is my son Abdul.

MR SHAH. Asalaam-a-lekum.

ABDUL. Walekum-a-salaam.

GEORGE. Tariq.

MR SHAH. Asalaam-a-lekum.

TARIQ. Walekum-a-salaam.

GEORGE. Maneer.

MR SHAH. Asalaam-a-lekum.

MANEER. Walekum-a-salaam.

ELLA (*calls*). Meenah. (*Enter* MEENAH.) Would you bring in the tea luv?

GEORGE. This is my daughter Meenah.

MEENAH (*posh*). Righty-ho (*She goes out to fetch the tea.*)

 Pause.

ELLA. Did you find it alright?

MR SHAH. Oh yes, no problem.

 Pause

 You have a very nice family, all boys, this is very good. God has blessed you.

ELLA. Well I could have done without so much blessing.

MR SHAH. I'm sorry?

ELLA. Doesn't matter. (*Changing the subject.*) Lovely frames you've got there.

MR SHAH. Yes, let me show you, these are my daughters, Nigget and Afsal-jaan. (*He passes them over, they're quite heavy.*)

ELLA. Oh they're quite hefty . . . the frames I mean! Look George, aren't they lovely?

SAJIT. Which one's Tariq's?

ELLA. Sit down cock, over there by the door.

GEORGE. Very nice photo. Where you buy frame like this?

MR SHAH. We had them especially made for our girls, gold leaf you know.

 Enter MEENAH *with the tea, she sees the photos. she can barely control her laughter, this could be dangerous. She scuttles out of the room quick.*

MEENAH. I'll just go and get the biscuits. (*She almost snorts this.*)

TARIQ *and* ABDUL *hear this but* ELLA *kills another outbreak with a look.*

MR SHAH. Do all your sons live at home?

ELLA *lights a fag,* MR SHAH *looks on disapprovingly.*

ELLA. All except Nazir, he's the eldest.

GEORGE. He travelling salesman.

SAJIT *moves closer to* MR SHAH, *he does a large twitch.*

MR SHAH. Erm. And this must be your youngest. (*To* SAJIT.) And how old are you?

SAJIT. Not old enough to get married, so don't ask me.

GEORGE (*veiled threat*). Sajit puther, go see if Saleem here yet.

MR SHAH. Ah yes, Saleem your college student, the engineer.

SAJIT. He's not, he's an artist, I've got a picture he drew of a . . .

SAJIT *is about to take out the picture* SALEEM *drew of a foreskin.* MANEER *retrieves it just in time.*

ABDUL. He means engineer . . . who erm paints engines Mr

Shah . . .

ELLA. Sajit. Saleem. Now. (SAJIT *gets the message and goes.*) Sorry about that Mr Shah he's erm . . . just been circumcised . . .

MR SHAH. Indeed.

ELLA. Where's that Meenah with them biscuits?

TARIQ. Shall I put the pictures of your daughters on the radiogram Mr Shah?

MR SHAH. So Tariq, do you have hobbies?

GEORGE. Only good ones. He like to work in shop most time.

Enter MEENAH *with biscuits.*

MEENAH. Would you like a biscuit, Mr Shah?

MR SHAH. Where did you get this sari?

MEENAH. Me Auntie Riffat in Pakistan.

MR SHAH. This is not what our women wear. You should wear Shalwar kameeze. It will look much better on you than this thing,

ELLA. Her Auntie Riffat said all women wear saris in Islamabad, and she's quite well to do, in't she George.

GEORGE. Riffat bloody stupy. (*To* MR SHAH.) Even in Pakistan women getting too bloody moderns.

MR SHAH. It's the government people I blame. They should set an example to the country.

ELLA. I think it looks lovely.

MR SHAH. It is not traditional dress in Pakistan.

GEORGE. Tradition see, Ella.

ANNIE (*off*). Youuu! Only me!

ANNIE *pokes her head round the door.*

ANNIE. Oh, I didn't know you had visitors. I won't stay long.

GEORGE. Annie, this is my friend Mr Shah, he daughters go be marry Abdul and Tariq.

ANNIE. Congratulations Mr Shah. (*Notices the pictures.*) Are these 'em? Oh, they look bleedin' gorgeous, you're lucky you two, landing a couple of belters like that.

GEORGE (*To* MR SHAH). Annie working for me since we first getting shop.

ELLA. I suppose you'll want tea now?

ANNIE. Seeing as you've asked me so bleeding politely I will.

ELLA. Meenah go and put the kettle on.

MEENAH *exits.*

ANNIE. Yeah they're lovely them, Mr Shah, you must be very proud of them. Beltin' frames as well.

MR SHAH. Yes, gold leaf you know.

ANNIE. I do know, I got something similar meself off the docks.

ELLA (*trying to shut her up*). Do you want a biscuit?

ANNIE. No ta. Three bob the pair they were. I've got a view of Kinder Scout in one and a three-dimensional of our lady in the other, looks beltin' don't it Ella?

MR SHAH. Mrs Khan . . .

ELLA. Call me Ella.

ANNIE. Everybody does.

MR SHAH. Erm . . . Mrs Khan, I am very proud that your sons are joining my family. (*This makes* ELLA *sit up and take note, even she knows it's the girls who are joining her family.*) I can see you have brought them up to be very respectful, which is very difficult in this day and age.

ANNIE. You're right there Mr Shah, they're a credit to her, and you George.

GEORGE. Oh yes, they good boys, no bring a trouble.

ANNIE. They'll do owt for you these two, you know last Whitsun they carried the banner of the Sacred Heart at a moment's notice, all the way from Regent Road t' town hall in Albert Square and back.

MR SHAH. What banner is this?

ANNIE. For the Whit week walks. Abdul and Tariq on the banner, Saleem, Maneer and our Clifford holding ribbons from the model of the holy sepulchre, with Sajit and Meenah chuckin' petals about in front.

GEORGE. Ella, what she bloody talking about?

MR SHAH (*slightly perturbed*). Is this a religious ceremony?

ANNIE. In a way I suppose you could say it was, but hardly anyone round 'ere's religious. It's just a day out f' kids and a new set of clothes.

ABDUL. We just helped out that once, lucky we were all there really.

Lights up on living room.

MEENAH. Brew up Twitch.

SAJIT. Get stuffed you fat cow!

MEENAH. I'll stuff you, you little twat!

MEENAH *flings herself and her sari over the sofa and onto* SAJIT. *He screams.*

Up on the parlour.

ELLA. Well you've got to lend a hand haven't you, I mean that's how we brought them up.

MR SHAH. But this was not their religion.

ANNIE (*digging herself out*). Well that's what a couple of belters you're getting, Mr Shah, they just jumped in there and gave help where help was needed, good Samaritans they were, just like in the Bible when . . .

We hear SAJIT *scream. This is a good time for* ELLA *to cut* ANNIE *off before she puts her foot in it again.*

ELLA. Tariq cock, will you go and see what they're up to? (*To* MR SHAH.) Kids eh? Were your two like that when they were younger?

TARIQ *exits.*

MR SHAH. No, my wife was a schoolmistress, she's always believed in firm discipline. Especially in a non-Pakistani environment.

ELLA. Oh I think you can be too harsh, don't you Annie?

ANNIE. Oh aye, yeah, mind you, our Peter knows how far he can go, before I knock him to kingdom come – and that's just me husband Mr Shah !

She bursts into laughter, ELLA *also but not as much as she would like.* GEORGE *and* MR SHAH *do not find it funny.*

ANNIE. Do you smoke Mr Shah? (*He declines, she gives one to* ELLA.) You could even say that in a Pakistani environment you'd still have to know where to draw the line with them, whereas with Ella and George they didn't have that environment, so they had to find their own line here in Salford, in this area among non-Pakistanis, but even without other Pakistanis they've got what you have as well, and done very well with it . . . like you have done. (*She's got to get out of this.*) You know they look just like you Mr Shah. (*Indicates the photos.*)

MR SHAH. Oh, no, no.

ELLA. She's right Mr Shah. They've got your eyebrows.

MR SHAH. I think there is a great preponderance placed on looks.

ANNIE. A what sorry?

GEORGE. 'Ponderance. (*To* MR SHAH.) What is latest news from East Pakistan?

Lights up on living room.

MEENAH. Have you seen them pictures though!

TARIQ. The one in the red looked like she had a hair-line that started from her eyebrows.

MEENAH. At least she had a neck. Our Abdul's looked like Smiffy out of the Bash Street Kids!

Enter MANEER *with a teapot.*

MANEER. Me mam said to hurry up with that tea.

TARIQ. What's going on in there?

MANEER. Me dad's building up to the war.

Up on the parlour.

GEORGE. Is bloody Indians see!

ANNIE. I'd better be going, got to go and see the undertaker about Scots Bertha, see you later George. Nice to meet you Mr Shah.

ELLA. See you later. (ANNIE *exits.*)

MR SHAH (*to* GEORGE). General Yahya Khan will hold the country together.

GEORGE. Ah yes, he's the man for that . . .

ELLA (*trying to make conversation*). Do your family come from Azad Kashmir, Mr Shah?

MR SHAH. My wife's family, mine are from Lahore, a beautiful city, the home of the arts in Pakistan. Have you been to Pakistan Mrs Khan?

ELLA. Never been asked.

MR SHAH. But you must go on holiday sometime, two months at least, see the whole country.

ELLA. Yeah, well, we can only manage two weeks in Rhyl. Even then George has to stay home and mind the shop.

MR SHAH. Really . . . well Pakistan is very different to Rhyl.

ELLA. Yeah right . . . it's got the sun for a start . . . have you been in England long Mr Shah?

MR SHAH. Since 1949. My wife studied here, in London, but later returned when my daughters were young. I don't think this is a fit society to bring up girls.

ELLA. All depends how you bring them up I think.

MR SHAH. But you have experienced only boys Mrs Khan.

ELLA. I've got Meenah as well Mr Shah.

MR SHAH. Yes this is true Mrs Khan, but . . . our girls are different.

ELLA (*does not like this*). Really.

GEORGE. Han, this is true, too much tickle-tackle go on see. You go to town, and you bloody see all bloody Indian girl. All bloody up to tickle-tackle with boy.

MR SHAH. This is the problem with our community, they
don't realise what a great danger it is to leave your children
to grow up in this country .

GEORGE. I been in this country since 1930, an' I telling you
no even bloody English same.

ELLA. What sort of work did you do when you first came Mr
Shah?

MR SHAH. Very degrading work I assure you Mrs Khan, very
degrading. I was over-qualified you see. First I swept the
floor in a mill, then I worked on the buses. Now I have four
butchers shops, two cars and a semi-detached house in
Trafford Park.

ELLA. Really?

MR SHAH. With double extensions.

ELLA. That's nice and roomy for you. Abdul go and see where
that tea is will you.

MR SHAH. My daughters both have their own bedrooms you
know. With Axminster carpet.

ELLA. Nice.

MR SHAH. They have attached bathrooms with same carpet.
My wife's idea.

ELLA. I've always found oil cloth better for the bathroom,
stops that smell of damp.

GEORGE. We have bathroom soon I think.

MR SHAH. How do you manage with so little room and so
many children Mrs Khan? It must be a bit of a squeeze.

ELLA. I've got three double beds and one single for Meenah.

MR SHAH. But where do you propose to put my daughters?

ELLA. One in the attic, the other on top of the chippy with
Abdul.

MR SHAH (*making his move*). But we have so much room at
our house, it seems such a shame to waste it. Would it not be
more convenient if your sons were to move in with us?

He looks to GEORGE *for agreement.*

ELLA. Erm, I thought the daughters-in-law moved in with their husband's family.

MR SHAH. But my daughters are used to modern conveniences. Perhaps when you get your bathroom fitted they may be able to move back. Though I'd have thought you'd be grateful for the extra space, I know I would be.

ELLA. But you don't know what you'd be getting yourself into Mr Shah. You've never experienced boys have you?

Up on living room.

ABDUL. Saj, go and see if Saleem's at Roy's.

SAJIT *runs out.*

ABDUL. Better not let him back in the parlour, Mr Shah thinks he's retarded.

MEENAH. He is.

TARIQ. Well if Sajit can't scare them off, nothing will.

ABDUL. You'd better hurry up and get changed, Mr Shah's waiting to meet you.

TARIQ. And if you're asked what you do at college you're an engineer who paints engines. Nowt to do with me, it was Twitch.

SALEEM (*to* SAJIT). You gobby little twat! (*Hits him.*)

TARIQ (*referring to model*). Is that it then?

MEENAH. It looks dead interesting that doesn't it Tariq?

TARIQ. Let's have a look at this great work of art then?

SALEEM *puts the model on the table, with its back to the audience, and lifts off the cover. The* OTHERS *look open mouthed.*

SALEEM. What do you think?

ABDUL. What are you gonna do with it?

SALEEM. I'm not gonna do anything with it, Abdul. It's an example of female exploitation in art.

MANEER. It looks disgusting.

TARIQ. I wouldn't say that.

MANEER. It's perverted.

MEENAH. Not even Twitch would do something like that.

SALEEM. It's art, you pillocks.

ELLA enters, muttering 'Axminster my arse', she does not see the model.

ELLA (*to* MEENAH). Oi you, where's that bleeding tea, get a move on, your dad's waiting for it. Abdul, Tariq parlour. (*To* SALEEM.) Hurry up and get ready, you should have been back half an hour ago. Sajit where'd you put those fags?

SALEEM. I said I was going for me model.

ELLA. Show me later, I haven't time now. (*She makes to go.*)

SAJIT. He's got a woman's fanny in a box mam!

The model is of a vagina complete with pubic hair.

ELLA. You dirty little bastard!

SALEEM. Mam, it's art.

ELLA. I'll art you, you little sod, I'll burn the bleeding thing.

ELLA goes to grab the model, but SALEEM *gets there first. She begins to chase him round the room.*

ELLA. Give it me!

SALEEM. Art's changed, mam.

ELLA. Aye and I'll change it some more when I get me hands on it.

We see her chase him into the hallway, followed by the OTHERS.

Up on parlour.

We are aware of the commotion outside the parlour door.

SALEEM (*from outside*). Mam let go, you're pulling all the hair out! Maam!

SALEEM *falls through the door clutching the model. He lands in front of* MR SHAH.

MR SHAH. Arghhh!!

SALEEM. Mr Shah, I'm Saleem, I'm an art student . . . erm . . . engineer!

GEORGE. Up baster!

MR SHAH. What is this thing, move it, take it away from me!

ELLA *comes through the door, followed by the* OTHERS.

ELLA. I'm very sorry Mr Shah, it was an accident, the hair came off in me hands.

MR SHAH. This is an insult to me, and to my family! How can you allow your son to behave like this! I will never let my daughters marry into this jungly family of half-breeds!

ELLA. They may be half-bred, but at least they're not bleeding in-bred like those two monstrosities. (*Indicating the pictures.*)

GEORGE. Ella!

ELLA. Never mind 'Ella'. (*Back to* SHAH.) Who the frig do you think you are coming in here telling me my house isn't good enough for your daughters. Well your daughters aren't good enough for my sons or my house. And if I hear you say another word about my family, I'll put that fanny over your bastard head.

MR SHAH. How dare you speak to me like this!

GEORGE. Ella you stop now or I bloody killing you!

MR SHAH. I won't stay here another minute, your wife is a disgrace!

ELLA. Sling your bleeding hook, go on, piss off! (*She points to the pictures.*) And take Laurel and frigging Hardy with you.

MR SHAH *takes the photos and exits.*

GEORGE. You baster bitch, you insulting guest, bring bloody shame on family!

ELLA. You ought to be ashamed George, you're not getting these lads married, you're selling them off to the highest bidder. Who's gonna get Meenah? Someone with double glazing and a detached house!

GEORGE grabs ELLA, and pushes her to the floor, he starts to hit her.

MEENAH. Maam! Maam! Abdul stop him!

SALEEM and TARIQ run over to try and stop him, MANEER grabs ELLA and tries to pull her away. SAJIT takes off his coat, runs over, and starts to hit GEORGE with it.

ABDUL. Dad! (*He grabs GEORGE and pushes him against the wall.*) Get off her stop it.

SALEEM. Smack him one Abdul!

ABDUL. Dad if you touch her again I swear I'll kill you!

GEORGE. You don't talk . . .

ABDUL. No dad, it's over, alright, it's finished!

SAJIT is still hitting him with his parka.

ABDUL. Sajit stop it!

SAJIT carries on hitting GEORGE.

ABDUL. I said stop it!

SAJIT stops and runs off to the shed crying. Pause. There's just the sound of ELLA crying. The OTHERS help her into a chair.

ABDUL. Just calm down dad, alright?

GEORGE starts to cry.

GEORGE. I only try to help you son, I no want to bloody hurt you, I love my family. I have to bloody stick up for family when people calling.

ABDUL. Go on over to the shop, go on, I'll come over in a bit.

GEORGE *looks at* ELLA *and the* OTHERS, *he looks at* ABDUL. *Ashamed and upset, he walks slowly out of the room.*

MEENAH. Don't cry mam, it wasn't your fault. Maneer, go and make some tea.

SALEEM. You should have stopped him from hitting her, Abdul.

TARIQ. Leave him out of it, Saleem.

ABDUL. I couldn't hit me dad.

SALEEM. Dad, that bastard's not a father, I don't know 'bout holding him back, you should've broken his neck.

ABDUL. What I did or didn't do has got fuck all to do with you Saleem.

SALEEM. Feeling guilty now are you?

ELLA. Just pack it in the lot of you, you get on me nerves. I can't do anything to please you, if it's not you it's your dad, if it's not your dad it's you. You're nothing but bleeding trouble. And (*To* SALEEM.) Pablo bleeding Picasso, that 'bastard' you've just been talking about is my husband, and whatever you may think of him he's still your father. So if I hear another foul-mouth word from anyone I'll have you. Now where's Sajit?

Enter MANEER *with the tea.*

MANEER. He's in the shed.

ABDUL. He took his parka off though, he hit me dad with it, when he slapped you.

ELLA. I don't believe it, I spend a year trying to get him out of that bloody coat, your dad hits me, and he whips it off and tries to kill him with it. I'll go have a word with him.

ELLA goes to the shed.

SALEEM. She's just gonna leave it, isn't she?

TARIQ. What else do you expect her to do?

SALEEM. She'll just let him walk back in here after what he's done?

MEENAH. He did after Nazir left didn't he.

SALEEM. So you're just gonna sit there, with your heads in the sand, until it happens again?

ABDUL. No one's hiding. Me mam's just trying to hold her family together.

SALEEM. Family! This isn't a family! Normal families sit down and talk. We say something out of line, me dad hits us and that's it.

ABDUL. It's not as simple as that, and you know it.

SALEEM. She should divorce him.

ABDUL. You're all missing the point, have you not thought that she might love him?

MEENAH. Me dad?

ABDUL. What else do you think has kept them together for so long? We're the cause of most of the arguments between them, 'cause she always takes our side.

TARIQ. So what do we do now, Abdul?

ABDUL. Try and make things easier for her, don't make her job any harder than it is. It's me dad that's gonna have to change.

MANEER. He was only trying to show us our culture.

ABDUL. He's got no right to tell us what our culture should be, he lost that when he settled here and married me mam.

MEENAH. God Abdul, you sound dead different.

SALEEM. Say that when you get married off.

ABDUL. That's not gonna happen to her, it's not gonna happen to anyone who doesn't want it. I'm telling you, things are gonna be different round here.

He picks up SAJIT'*s coat from the floor and goes to the yard.*

MEENAH. 'Kinell.

ABDUL *meets* ELLA *in the sitting room.*

ELLA. He's all yours. I want to go over and see your dad in a bit, we've got to talk, will you come with me?

ABDUL. Course I will.

ELLA *gives* ABDUL *a hug. This is quite awkward as they're not a physical family.*

ABDUL. Thanks for sticking up for us mam.

ELLA (*pulling away*). Go on you big daft get, go give him his coat.

ABDUL *goes into the yard.*

ABDUL. Sajit are you still in there?

SAJIT. Get stuffed you!

ABDUL. What have I done?

SAJIT. You shouted at me for hitting me dad.

ABDUL. I know, I'm sorry, come out I want to talk to you.

SAJIT *emerges slowly.*

SAJIT. I was only hitting him 'cause he hit me mam. He always does it. He said he was gonna burn the house down.

ABDUL. You don't have to worry about that, I won't let him. Here I've brought your parka.

SAJIT. I didn't half give him a belt didn't I?

ABDUL (*smiling*). Yeah, do you want it or what?

SAJIT. No.

ABDUL. Stick it in the bin then.

SAJIT *takes the coat, goes over to the bin, lifts up the lid, takes one last look at his coat, and throws it in.*

SAJIT. Abdul.

ABDUL. Yeah?

SAJIT. Can I have another look at our Saleem's model?

ABDUL (*laughing*). No!

The end.

This revised edition of *East is East* first published
in Great Britain in 1997 as a paperback original
by Nick Hern Books Ltd, 14 Larden Road, London W3 7ST
in association with the Royal Court Theatre, London

First edition published as an Instant Playscript
by Nick Hern Books, 1996

Front cover: Linda Bassett and Imran Ali in the first
production. Photo by Robert Day

Typeset by Country Setting, Woodchurch, Kent, TN26 3TB
Printed by Cox and Wyman Limited, Reading, Berks

ISBN 1 85459 313 7

A CIP catalogue record for this book is available from
the British Library